Become "Street Wise"

A Woman's Guide To Personal Safety

by
Arthur Cohen

Published by Target Consultants International Ltd.
P.O. Box 463 • Massapequa Park, New York 11762

Target Consultants International Ltd.

TABLE OF CONTENTS

About the author

As one of the nation's leading advocates of crime prevention education, Arthur Cohen has established himself as a voice of reason for safety and awareness education. Crime/rape prevention and awareness education is a mandatory survival skill.

A sought after speaker, he is both a motivational and inspirational force on a wide range of crime prevention and safety programs. His presentations reflect the experience, knowledge and excitement gathered from 25 years in public education and 30+ years experience in self defense and crime prevention study. His program "Become Streetwise!" A Woman's Guide To Personal Safety is perhaps the leader in the field and has received praise from educators, health and law enforcement professionals from around the country.

Arthur's background includes serving as a staff instructor for the American Society of Law Enforcement Trainers, the P.P.C.T. International Police Instructor's Conference, the Justice System Training Association and the Police Self Defense Instructors International. In addition, he made several appearances on Law Enforcement Television Network and was included in Who's Who in Law Enforcement Trainers in 1988. He is president of Target Consultants International a group of over 200 police trainers and instructors providing crime/rape prevention education to the public in over 20 states and Australia.

A 5th Degree Black Belt in Tae Kwon Do with over 30 years of training, he achieved international recognition as a result of his books, training videos, articles, demonstrations and seminars and is listed in Who's Who in Karate and Who's Who in American Martial Arts.

A master story teller, he speaks from personal experience to educate, motivate, inspire and entertain. Recent recognition of his accomplishments has resulted in his being included in the American Seminar Leaders Association's Speakers Bureau and Who's Who in Seminar Leaders.

ACKNOWLEDGMENT

There are many dedicated professionals who have made contributions to the field of rape prevention. Untold hours were spent to compile and analyze statistics and put together articles, books and pamphlets for the public's safety. I have utilized dozens of these works and would like to acknowledge all of them. Many are to be found in the bibliography at the back of this work.

I would also like to thank the many people who appeared in both the book and slide show.

Special thanks to Gary Birnhak and Michael Schwartz for their special effort with the photography. I would like to thank Sy Grudko, Eileen Tully, Jim Michaud and Stephanie Hahn for the cartooning. It made the slide show and book very special.

And the outstanding cover was done by Joe Howard.

Without Charles Barrett of Charles Barrett Graphics Inc., the project might have taken twice as long and only been half as good. He gave us everything and I appreciate it.

Ms. Susan Bruno, came through as usual, and Mrs. Olivia Salina helped with their proof-reading specialty. Thanks ladies.

Last but not least, I would like to thank Dr. James Brucia, School Superintendent, and the Massapequa Public Schools for their confidence and support.

INTRODUCTION

All one has to do is pick up a newspaper to see how crime has become part of our lives. Muggings, rapes, assaults and even murders are now commonplace throughout our society. In many areas, citizens fear leaving their homes or apartments after dark. It is no longer safe using many parks and public places or even in your car. The police and society can no longer provide us with the security we need. Many of the robbers are not just content to rob, but seem to have a callous disregard for their victims. They will inflict pain and punishment when there seems no need or purpose for it. The once-safe suburbs are now experiencing the crimes that were reserved for the cities. For whatever reason these assaults occur, be they drug-related, due to the economy or societal pressures, the victim pays the price.

While almost no one would refute that there is a need for more rape prevention training, very few individuals seem to find the time in their busy schedules to actually learn more about the subject. In fact, it has always been puzzling why women think it is important for "other women" to have this knowledge, but they themselves fail to take advantage of a similar opportunity. But looking at the statistics, it becomes increasingly clear that rape prevention is a topic that should concern all women. And men as well.

QUESTION: WHAT CAN A PERSON DO ?

Actually, quite a bit. First, become aware of the problem. Second, try to find ways to eliminate or reduce risks. That is the purpose of this booklet and seminar. We will make you aware of things you probably did not know about or think of. Also, we will make suggestions on how to change the way you act or function. But, in the final analysis, it is you who are most important. Will a little work or inconvenience deter you? We certainly hope not.

It is possible that many women feel they are well informed on the subject of rape and sexual assault. They know enough about the subject that it could never happen to them. We'll see. Take the *"Rape Quiz"* and compare what you know with the experts.

Rape Quiz

Ans. ____ 1. What are the chances that a woman will be a victim of a sexual assault in her lifetime ?
a. 1 in a 1000 *b. 1 in a 100*
c. 1 in 50 *d. 1 in 3*

Ans. ____ 2. Where do the greatest number of rapes occur?
a. Home or apartment *b. Dark alley*
c. Park or beach *d. A car*

Ans. ____ 3. The rape victim is selected because
a. She is young and good looking.
b. She is alone and vulnerable.
c. She provoked the attack.
d. She dressed in a manner to provoke the attack?

Ans. ____ 4. How long does the average rape last?
a. 20-40 minutes *b. 40-60 minutes*
c. 1-2 hours *d. 2-4 hours*

Ans. ____ 5. What percentage of rapes are ever reported?
a. 10% *b. 50%* *c. 75%* *d. 90%*

Ans. ____ 6. What percentage of the time does the victim and the rapist know each other?
a. 10% *b. 25%* *c. 50%* *d. 90%*

Ans. ____ 7. The youngest rape victim reported was about
a. 10 years old *b. 5 years old.*
c. 2 years old. *d. 3 months old*

Ans. ____ 8. The oldest rape victim reported was about
a. 75 years old *b. 85 years old.*
c. 95 years old *d. 100 years old*

Ans. ____ 9. What percentage of women complies with a rapist's demands even though no physical force is used (verbal threats only)?
a. 10% *b. 25%* *c. 50%* *d. 75%*

Ans. ____ 10. What percentage of rapes occur in a dating situation?
a. 10% *b. 25%* *c. 50%* *d. 75%*

THE 10 BIGGEST LIES ABOUT RAPE AND SEXUAL ASSAULT

Due to the limited and bias sources of information available to the public, there are a number of myths or "lies" that are commonly believed about rapes / sexual assault. The following information was part of an article submitted to a woman's magazine in the hope of educating women and the public.

IT CAN'T HAPPEN TO ME.

In 1991 over 238,000 rapes were reported to police. According to a survey done by the Justice Department, the number of rape victims was over 600,000. In many of the private surveys taken, it appears only one in ten sexual assaults are actually reported. So, while no woman wants to believe she will be a victim of rape/sexual assaults, it is a fact that women are being sexually assaulted in large numbers.

IT DOESN'T HAPPEN AROUND HERE.

Rape is probably one of the most under-reported of all crimes. The victim is often devastated by the assault and will usually keep the attack to herself. This is particularly true if the assault is a result of "date rape", the assaulter is a family member, friend of the family, etc. Victims are often afraid of being further victimized by a Criminal Justice System that seems to show more concern for the criminal than for the victim. The problem is that the trauma and pain do not easily disappear. Psychological scars could last a lifetime. More than most crimes, rape is frequently covered up to protect the reputation and "dignity" of a person, college, secondary school or other institution. When no physical damage is apparent, it is easy for someone to say "forget about what happened and get on with your life." The cover-up gives others a false sense of security. I can't tell you how many times I have been told,"We don't have a problem around here." Sometimes this statement is made out of ignorance but other times it is a conscious effort to conceal the truth. I know of no college that doesn't have a problem regardless of the location.

STATISTICS DON'T LIE.

"There are lies, damn lies and statistics." Statistics are used to create any atmosphere the group, organization or institution desires. The figures, though misleading, give credibility to the statements of the organization or institution. Two cases come to point. College security at one school told a student, "If you report the assault to the police they will come back and get you." This was clearly intended to cover-up the crime. How many other students were told similar stories? President Bush signed a bill in 1992 requiring the colleges throughout the country to submit crime statistics to the Justice Dept. Up to now, less than 10% were reporting them. But as we have seen, it is easy to manipulate the figures. Will we ever see an accurate accounting? There was one case reported where a college security director was fired for reporting the crime stats on campus to outsiders. How can students be alerted to the problem on campus if reporting is discouraged? Another case where a woman assaulted in the parking lot at a major mall was later told, "This was the first case brought to our attention." She was later to learn the mall had at least 80 reported assaults in the past 2-3 years. In reality, the malls are having a major problem maintaining safety for shoppers. This is also a well kept secret.

U.S. IS THE RAPE CAPITOL OF THE WORLD.

It is, if you believe the stats compiled by the Senate Judiciary Committee. According to the report, the U.S. has a rape rate 13 times higher than Britain, 4 times higher than Germany and 20 times higher than Japan. From my experience, in spite of it's flaws, crime reporting in the U.S. is probably the most accurate found in any country.

So, at first glance, it is impossible to compare our numbers with anyone else's. However, if we look deeper into the issue, we find our definition of rape is different than those used in other countries. I have been told by a high ranking Mexican Police Official, "There is no rape problem in Mexico." I have evidence of young girls in India being sold by their families to Arab buyers for hundreds or thousands of dollars. It is known that families in China will kill or discard female babies because they don't work as hard as males. When we see the rights of women at very low levels in Middle Eastern countries where they can not hold office or in some cases even drive a car, do you actually believe rape or sexual assault is going to be reported in an honest way? The world has a long way to catch up to the U.S. and we have a long way to go.

SOCIETY IS VERY CONCERNED ABOUT THE PROBLEM OF RAPE AND SEXUAL ASSAULT.

If a survey were taken, we would undoubtedly find no one in support of rape or sexual assaults on women. However, action speaks louder than words. If concern is measured by action and ways of preventing women from being assaulted, then, in my opinion, society is not concerned enough. Would we be concerned if 600,000 people a year were injured in accidents or caught a disease? You bet we would. Either safety programs or vaccines would be administered to correct these problems. Why is that effort not going into crime/rape prevention programs in the public schools? Why haven't the politicians and educational leaders started programs? Why are the number of assaults on women found buried in the paper while other things find their way to the front page? It is well documented by psychologists and psychiatrists that rapists are repeaters and can not be cured. Why then aren't these "predators" locked away for longer periods or given counseling programs that will help them cope with their problem? It is well known that the average criminal will serve only about one third of his sentence. Isn't rape serious enough to keep these people off the streets? A repeatedly convicted rapist should be given life with no chance of parole. Why is he allowed to return to society and repeat his crime time and again? When judges make comments like "boys will be boys", what message is that sending out? Maybe it is time for society to get off its double standard regarding sex and individuals' rights.

IT'S A FREE COUNTRY; I CAN GO ANYWHERE I WANT.

"Looks like dinner is here"

I hear this comment quite frequently. Some women confuse living in a democracy with living in an environment where criminals search and wait for unsuspecting victims. Anyone has a right to go where and when they please. That's what the zebra said when it went to feed on the choicest grass in the field near where lions were resting. The lion wasn't going to discourage the zebra. The lion was only thinking how tasty zebra would be for dinner. Know this for a fact, the criminal is an opportunist, he/she/they are out there constantly on the lookout for easy prey. The research clearly indicates that many victims provided the criminal with an optimum opportunity for being successful. Where and when we travel can make the difference and provide the criminal with easy pickings. I don't see many people swimming in shark infested waters; they have a right to you know.

NOTHING WILL HAPPEN TO ME "I AM STREETSMART".

This is the very attitude that could get you into trouble. The average person is no match for the average criminal. We can say what we want about criminals but they are working at getting better at what they do. If they are not good at their performance, some are caught, and a few even go to jail. However, while in jail the criminal is provided with a learning environment that will make him wiser and probably more vicious before he's released (graduates). For many criminals going to jail is advanced education. Few members of the public are a match for the ingenuity and viciousness of the criminal. "Quality"crime/rape prevention education designed by professionals in crime prevention, is a must for anyone and should be included as part of the public education system.

NOT TO WORRY "SOCIETY IS GETTING 'TUFF' ON CRIME".

These are statements usually associated with political candidates on the campaign trail. However, the truth of the matter is the courts are overwhelmed and the jails are overcrowded. Sexual predators are known repeaters, they are seldom caught, they are hard to convict and they are frequently released after serving a fraction of their sentenced time. Society doesn't appear ready to put its money where its' mouth is. The cost of doing it right is astronomical. When asked about the cure for the crime problem, one criminal justice expert was quoted as saying "I don't know the cure; it looks like society might have to learn to live this way." This is a horrible indictment of our democratic system.

STIFFER JAIL TERMS WILL DETER RAPISTS.

In the past, rape was one of the least reported crimes. Also, it was one of the most difficult to get a conviction on. Very often, a plea bargain approach was used by prosecutors to get rapists off the streets, even if for a short period of time. Thankfully, things are improving. However, a frightening picture has been appearing about the nature of rape and the rapist. The experts, sociologists, and psychologists have started to tell us that rapists can't be cured. At best, a rapist with the desire and proper counseling can learn to control his urge to rape. When given the opportunity, very few rapists are opting for this counseling program . Not many appear to have a desire to change their behavior. The proof of the matter is rapists have been caught raping while out on bail, on parole and even immediately after being released. The problem is so serious and frustrating that the State of Washington has enacted a "Sexual Predator Law." This law will prevent a select group of brutal repeat sexual offenders from ever being released from jail. Presently, this law is being tested in the courts for its' constitutionality. It appears at this time, the solution for dealing with sexual crime offenders has yet to be found. However, it doesn't appear the fear of stiff jail sentences is much of a deterrent.

NOTHING CAN BE DONE TO REDUCE A WOMAN'S CHANCES OF BEING A VICTIM.

Nothing can be further from the truth. God helps those who help themselves. The first step is getting a good education about the problem. Crime/rape prevention education is a positive first step. A good program should begin with a pro-active approach using sound education principles. The program should stress avoiding the negative and accentuating the positive. Knowing how the criminal thinks and acts will be useful in defeating his/her or their plan. Learn when to fight and how to fight. Also, know when not to fight. Prevention and awareness, passive resistance and active resistance are all tools to be used appropriately. Proper education and training in their use is essential to a successful outcome. Any instructor advocating fighting back without looking into the nature of the victim, the assaulter and the surrounding environment where the attack occurs is not necessarily giving the best advice. A plan of action is most important before action is taken. Physically fighting back should be the last step when no other possibilities exist. I recognize this recommendation is not what some people would like to hear; however, it does save wear and tear on the body.

RAPE

AND

OTHER CRIMES

AGAINST WOMEN

TOTAL NUMBER OF RAPES

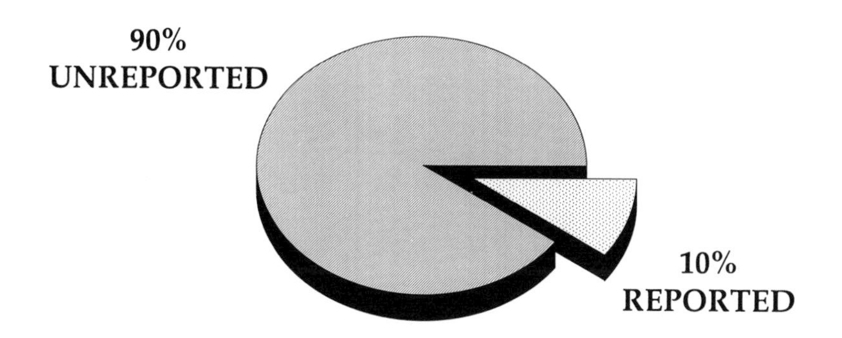

Over 207,000 forcible rapes were reported in 1991, according to the FBI. Most police sources concur that only ***10% of all rapes are ever reported***; if this is accurate, the actual number of rapes is closer to 2,000,000 for the year. Reported rape is noticeably on the rise. Rape and other violent assaults on women have become a problem of epidemic proportions. FBI projections suggest that as many as ***1 out of 3*** women can expect to be sexually assaulted in their lifetime. And according to the Department of Justice, 3 out of 4 women will be the victim of a violent crime during their lifetime.

Recently, a judge who was hearing a rape charge against a teenage boy was quoted in the paper as saying, "He was just sowing some wild oats." Rape is not some inconsequential "sowing of wild oats," but a major violent crime. And rape is not just a woman's problem, but a problem of our society, and society must come to grips with it. One way is to eliminate the double standard that most of us were brought up with concerning what a man could do and what a woman could do. Also, the health education program in public schools should educate young people about the rights of all people, both male and female, concerning their bodies. However, until society wakes up to its responsibilities, you must take measures to help yourself.

A recent study financed by the National Institute of

COLLEGE WOMEN INTERVIEWED

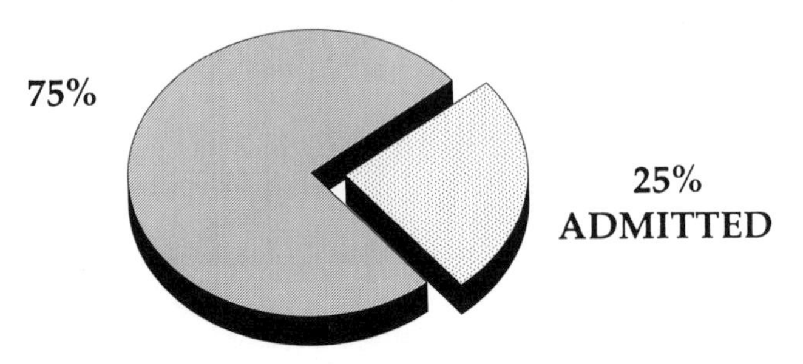

Mental Health interviewed about 7000 college women from schools across the country and the results were shocking.

* About 25 % of all college women have reported been raped.

* About 50 % of the rapes were by first dates or romantic friends.

* Most victims were aged 15-25 years of age.

* Over 90% did not report the incident.

* Over 90% knew their assailant.

QUESTION: WHY DOES SUCH A LARGE NUMBER OF RAPES GO UNREPORTED?

A number of varied reasons might account for this figure, such as:

* The victim, already traumatized, wants to avoid further stress and trauma. She only wants to forget and put the incident out of her mind.

Many victims are embarrassed. They are ashamed that

* their family or friends will learn about it. Many point accusing fingers and often blame the victim.

* Another problem is the rapist might be a family member or close "friend" of the family, or acquaintance. ***In about 50% of the cases the victim knows the rapist*** .

* The victim, wanting to keep family peace, keeps quiet. The cost is that she has to live with the experience. Frequently this takes its toll on the victim.

* The victim believes, or is led to believe by the rapist, that she was to blame for the assault or that she led him on. The victim, therefore, accepts some responsibility for the act.

* The victim fears reprisals from the rapist. Rapists often leave with a threat about coming back, etc. It has been found that seldom, if ever, does the rapist return to the victim.

* The victim fears going through the legal system. Our legal system, in its attempt to be fair to all , has some flaws in it. In the case of the rapist and victim, the system's failures are most apparent. The court process is long and often humiliating.

WHERE RAPES OCCUR

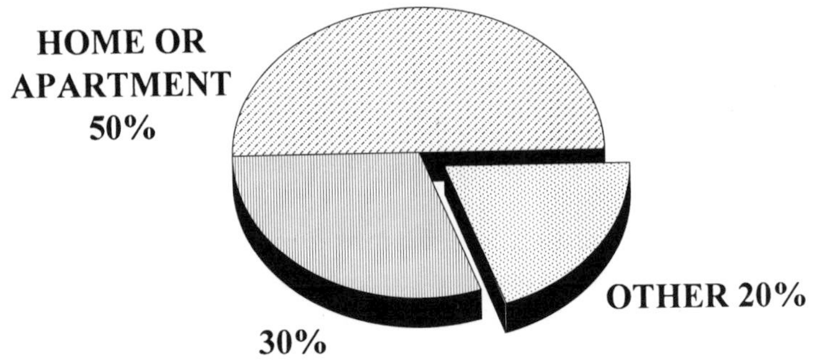

Rapes can occur almost anywhere. Almost 50% of reported rapes occur in the home: often the victim's, but sometimes the rapist's. The average rape ***lasts between 2-4 hours***, the shortest on record being about 20 minutes. Another popular spot for a rape is the automobile. Again, sometimes the victim's and sometimes the rapist's. Rapes have occurred in parks, restrooms, office buildings, airports and even jails. There are two key factors that appear to be essential for rape and they are:

1. Isolation
2. Uninterrupted period of time.

QUESTION: WHAT ARE THE FOUR STAGES OF RAPE?

Studies show that most rapes go through a definite series of stages.

STAGE ONE: During this stage the rapist tries to get control of his victim. He tries to intimidate by threats, grabbing, roughing up the victim, and/or brandishing a weapon. It is during this stage that the rapist will try to isolate the victim from a public area where his plans might be interrupted.

STAGE TWO: The rapist tries to get a sexual release. However, a percentage of rapists rarely receive sexual satisfaction. Many studies seem to indicate a percentage of rapists have a problem achieving sexual gratification. This is now blamed on the victim and leads to stage three.

STAGE THREE: During this stage the rapist will beat, possibly cut, and try to inflict various kinds of pain and punishment on the person he feels is responsible for his failure to achieve gratification. It is the victim's screams and terror that allows the rapist to reach fulfillment.

STAGE FOUR: This stage occurs in only a small percentage of rape cases: less than 5%. This is the psychotic rapist who will retaliate against the victim. In his warped mind he sees the victim as the reason for his acting out the rape scenario. At this point he becomes so enraged and out of control that he will repeatedly stab and bludgeon the victim. When this happens in a community, panic sets in.

RAPE IS A POWER TRIP

NOT A PASSION TRIP

QUESTION: WHAT CAN BE DONE TO DETER OR DEFEND AGAINST A STALKER?

The term stalker is used to identify an individual who repeatedly follows, tries to contact, harasses or intimidates others.

The current research classifies the stalkers into the following groups:

Psychopathic Personality Stalker

* Almost always male
* Fully aware of the nature of his actions
* Will exhibit a hypermacho facade to hide inner feelings of inferiority
* Comes from an abusive family background where violence was the norm
* Generally he targets a wife or ex-girlfriend
* Control freaks who use stalking as a means to regain control of lost "love"

Ruth Micklem, co-director of Virginians Against Domestic Violence says "Nearly one third of all women killed in America are murdered by their husbands or boyfriends, and as many as 90% of them have been stalked." (Newsweek. July 13, 1992)

Psychotic Personality Stalker

* Can be male or female

* Many have a clearly defined mental disorder

Psychotic Personality Stalker

* Can be male or female

* Many have a clearly identifiable mental disorder i.e. paranoia, schizophrenia etc.

* They will appear normal/sane in daily life when not pursuing their target

* They become obsessed with the target, usually a stranger

* A subgroup of this type is the erotomania. Their erotic delusion is fed by the notion that they are loved by the target

* This group usually targets persons of higher social status i.e. public figures, actors, actresses, politicians

In the past, law enforcement has found it particularly difficult to deal with this group of criminal until it was too late. However, new anti-stalking legislation has been passed in over 20 states. The new legislation places the responsibility on the stalker to prove he/she did not intend to scare, frighten or endanger the victim. We are dealing with a relatively new phenomenon and are learning on a try as you go basis. There doesn't appear to be unanimous agreement on the part of the "experts" as to the most effective intervention. However, all agree that stalkers pose a serious threat and should be taken seriously. Stalkers are to be considered dangerous. In addition, stalkers are not easily discouraged. Many have been known to continue their harassment even after serving months or years in jail.

If you think you are the target of a stalker, this is what the experts suggest:

* Take it seriously

* Document and date every act regardless of how funny or innocent i.e. love notes, candy, flowers etc.

* Contact police ASAP once you realize that this is something out of the ordinary. Don't delay!

MEET

THE RAPIST:

HE IS EVERYWHERE

QUESTION: THE RAPIST, WHAT IS HE?

In the movies, we can almost always pick out the rapist. He seems to stand out in the crowd. Unfortunately, the reality of the situation is much to the contrary. On the surface, the rapist often appears to be normal in almost all aspects of daily life. However, low self-esteem is a common denominator among all types of rapists. He seems to have a feeling of frustration which is somewhat satisfied by brutally bullying a smaller, helpless person. As a group, they have a high rate of sexual dysfunction during rape incidents. They also appear to have poorly developed heterosexual skills. Studies seem to indicate that many rapists were sexually abused as children. For some rapists, sexual gratification is a factor. This would probably be the type a individual know as the exploitive rapist. However for others, sex is not the motivating factor, instead it is the choice of expression. The rapist is a walking weapon, driven by uncontrolled hostility or a quest for power and he enjoys watching women being frightened. A repeater by his own admission, he would probably do it again once he is out of jail, according to many who were surveyed.

All rapists are not alike. A response that might effectively deter one rapist, might only serve to anger another. A master of emotion, he might appear as polite, helpful and charming, trying to con the victim into a vulnerable position. Or he might be menacing and threatening , hoping to intimidate the victim into a situation that he can totally control. This requires isolating the victim where he can proceed without interruption. While rapists of all ages have been documented, they seem to concentrate between 16 and 25 years of age. No ethnic group seems to monopolize the greatest percentage. They seem to be equally divided between white and black. However, in the black areas rapists and victims tend to be black and in the white areas, rapists and victims tend to be white. This is contrary to a popular myth that rapists of one ethnic group prey on victims from another group. In most cases, the rapist and the victim are from the same ethnic group.

TYPES OF RAPISTS

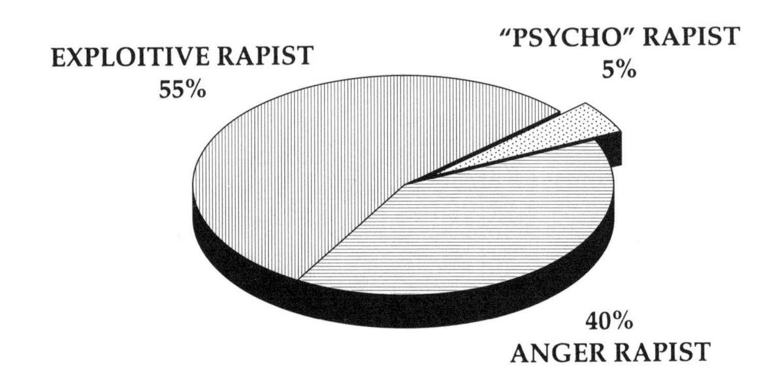

There appear to be three characteristic groups of rapists. They are:

1. The Exploitive Rapist (Approx. 55% of the total)
He sees woman as an object for sexual gratification. Rape is a spur of the moment event. This is generally characterized as the "date rapist" and likely to be an outgrowth of a social situation. The rapist cannot believe a women can possibly say no. He perceives a woman's resistance as a sexual ploy and this often heightens sexual arousal. Often the rapist is socially immature and has difficulty reading body language, thereby misinterpreting a woman's "no." Sexual release is a factor with the exploitive rapist.

2. The Anger Rapist (Approx. 40% of the total)
Rape is just an expression of misplaced anger and hostility, and sex is his way to humiliate his victim. The victim represents a hated female figure. (Example. ex-wife, girl friend or mother.) Fighting back is likely to increase this rapist's rage. This rapist has a poor self-image and is obsessed with sexual

fantasies. He feels that no woman in her right mind would have sex with him. He often fantasizes his victim's falling in love with him.

3. The Sadistic or "Psycho" Rapist (Approx. 5% of the total) Fortunately, this rapist is in the minority. He is the most violent and dangerous of all rapists. As a group they are the most likely to use weapons. He finds pleasure in inflicting pain. Often the assaults are pre-meditated. Sexual feelings and aggression are fused. The sadistic rapist often acts out his fantasy in a type of ritualized game. This game often ends in the death of the victim. Jack the Ripper and Richard Speck are two classic examples and a number of murdered victims are attributed to each. He is the most difficult to catch and prosecute because there are no witnesses.

All rapists are potentially dangerous and violent. In a recent study of sex offenders on probation, some interesting insights into the mind of the rapist and how he perceives the world have appeared. This is what the investigations were able to obtain from the rapists:

1. Women are seducers.
2. Women mean yes when they say no.
3. The rape really wasn't a big thing .
4. Nice girls don't get raped.

According to the interviewer, about 1/3 continue to deny the act. Some admit the act, but deny it was rape. They suggest the victims led them on. In cases where the molesting of young children is involved, the molester was either a relative, friend or neighbor of the victim. About 60% admitted molesting, while about 40% continue to deny it. In cases of child abuse, very few gave a good reason for it, but, interestingly enough, very few showed remorse; possibly indicating that they will repeat the crime. Bear in mind that this was a small study and, thus, it is dangerous to make blanket generalizations.

Punishment does not appear to be much of a deterrent to a rapist. Like a drug addict, he is not in control of his actions. The only saving grace is that jail does remove him from circulation. But, the bad news is that it is usually for too short a period. And as seen, he will usually go back to the same old habits. Police statistics seem to substantiate this statement. Society has not yet found a solution for this type of criminal. An extensive counseling and rehabilitation program must be undergone before rapists should ever be allowed to leave prison. Just serving time is not sufficient.

Multiple rape has been on the rise in a number of areas. In about 25% of the rapes, two rapists were involved. Victims are seldom killed. And, in many cases, the victim is not physically harmed. It is possible multiple attackers can do what one attacker finds difficult, controlling the victim. It could be that they have overwhelming force to control and intimidate the victim, and it is not necessary to do more. Finally, the rapist might be concerned that there would be witnesses to the murder, the other rapist. Rapists realize there is a good chance of getting away with rape. However, murder is another story altogether. In some instances, we are seeing an increase in the senseless violence used against women. The Central Park Jogger Case, which received national attention, typefies this senseless violence.

RAPE: THE VICTIM

QUESTION: WHO IS THE VICTIM?

A dramatic increase in women living alone, and more women in the work force working odd hours, have placed women in vulnerable positions. Every female is a potential victim. Reports of victims ranging in age from ***a few months*** to well ***into their 90's*** have been documented. All races have been targeted, but it appears that the group most at risk is black women living in the ghetto. Most vulnerable is the woman living alone. ***Vulnerability and opportunity*** are two of the key factors. Another important factor is the woman who is unsure of herself and lacks confidence. She becomes an easy mark. A further important factor is the woman who is not alert when she travels in public. Together, the uncertain and the unaware comprise what is often termed "victim mentality."

PROFILE OF A "VICTIM MENTALITY"

1. Easily Distracted - Individual has a low awareness level, tendency to daydream in public.

2. Lack of Self - Confidence - Individual has a poor self-image reflected in her walk and body language.

3. Easily Intimidated - Individual will usually succumb to verbal threats only. Studies indicate that about 50% of all victims complied with a rapist's demands even though no physical force was used.

4. Overly Trusting - Individual will accept any story at face value without checking its authenticity. Will allow a repairman into her home because he wears work clothes.

5. Wreckless - Individual is willing to take unnecessary risks. These might include dangerous shortcuts, staying out late at night, going home with men she just met, bar hopping, etc.

If you feel you fit into one or more of the five categories, then there is room for improvement; and improvement can be achieved. However, I did not say it would be easy. Remember, it took you years to develop into the person you are. Read the sections on the benefits of exercise and the benefits of martial arts training. I have seen both men and women, young and old, change dramatically through the benefits of martial arts training.

REMEMBER: MOST ATTACKERS WANT A VICTIM, NOT A FIGHT.

QUESTION: WHAT DOES BODY LANGUAGE HAVE TO DO WITH BEING A VICTIM?

Body language is a way of talking without speaking. We are constantly telling people something about ourselves, sometimes without knowing it or wanting to. Often a poor self-image will be reflected in certain gestures that an attacker would pick up on.

How do you walk: with a sign of insecurity or an air of confidence? When you speak with someone, do you look him in the eye or down on the floor? These all reflect the confidence level of a woman. It has been found that personality can be changed by changing your body language. A person can develop more confidence after learning appropriate body language.

Also, changing the image a woman has about herself will go far to change the way she walks and carries herself.

NO SHOULD MEAN NO!

But unfortunately, it doesn't always seem to be the case. We live a society of double standards, not just the United States, where men are led to believe that women are available for their pleasure or convenience. There has been some movement to change this attitude, but there is a long road ahead.

We don't want to brand all men as predators but there are many out there. Some men will stop after a firm no while others might not. There are some who don't believe, no means no. And then there is a group of 'sickos' , not motivated by sexual pleasure, that have already made their plans, and little or nothing will deter them from completing an act of violence against a vulnerable woman.

DOUBLE MESSAGES

For aggressive males, that will stop if properly handled, it is important to be sure that there is no chance they misinterpret the signals. Mixed signals confuse people and lead to misunderstandings. Often victims question the signals they gave and place the blame on themself. We want to avoid this. Be sure your verbal messages and body language give the same clear message in unmistakable terms. We don't want to have a bad situation come down because there was a breakdown in communication. Rapists sometimes use this as an excuse. Although, many rapists have difficulty reading no messages. So don't be afraid to set limits in a way that can not be misunderstood.

QUESTION: WHY ME?

A question that often plagues a victim is "Why did this happen to me?" In addition to any physical damage, the victim of a crime carries emotional and psychological wounds. Victims of sex crimes seem to have the most severe mental consequences.

According to Syeve Berglas, a clinical psychologist who conducts stress treatment programs at McLean Hospital-Harvard Medical School, the victim usually goes through 3 distinct stages:

Stage 1 is characterized by a breakdown of normal functioning. This lasts for hours or days. Many are so paralyzed with shock and/or disbelief, they often can't report the crime to police. Denial is typical and is characterized by the statement "This can't be happening to me."

During **Stage 2**, the victim tries to recover from the initial shock. She may experience fantasies, dreams or nightmares. In addition, she can experience a wide range of emotions that might include apathy, anger, rage and/or anxiety. Many, especially victims of battering, rape or incest, can experience long periods of traumatic depression. Often during periods of depression, victims will blame themselves. If it continues too long, self-blame can shatter their self-image and threaten their long term emotional adjustment. Withdrawal is often a consequence of blaming oneself.

In **Stage 3**, the victim comes to grips with the experience and begins to channel mental and physical energy into more positive areas. A study by psychiatric Nurse Ann Burgess of the University of Pennsylvania and sociologist Lynda Holmstrom of Boston College, clearly showed that victims of rape who received social support recovered much more quickly. We would probably find similar results for recovering victims of other crimes.

According to many experts, a key to regaining self-esteem is learning how to be less vulnerable to crime. As a crime prevention advocate, I have been trying to get this important message across to the public and the educational institutions in this country. Wouldn't it make sense to provide crime prevention education to everyone before they become victims?

UNDERSTANDING THE VICTIM

All rape victims do not react the same to their experience. Although all are not hurt physically, they all suffer some psychological trauma. One minute the woman is feeling confident and good about herself and the next minute all of this is gone. Often, the stronger the woman was before, the greater the change after.

It has been found that those women who offered resistance have a better time recovering from the psychological effects of rape than those who did not. It is believed that those who offered no resistance blame themselves for not doing more to prevent the crime. In my experience in studying animal an human behavior and teaching self-defense for over thirty years, I have found that a percentage of the population, both male and female, respond to assault by freezing. It is not a decision made in the conscious mind. It is a subconscious choice we have little control over. It might be likened to certain animals freezing to avoid being noticed by predators. It is unfortunate that some women blame themselves for this behavior because I believe they had little choice.

Some of the ways victims respond to rape are:

* Severe shock
* Fear
* Anger and rage
* Guilt and shame - Did I encourage this? Why me?
* Loss of dignity, self-esteem and self-determination
* Feelings of being dirty and worthless
* Confusion

This often results in the following:

* Nightmares
* Washing and bathing almost ritualistically
* Loss of sexual feelings for a husband or boyfriend
* Withdrawal from friends and family
* Lost of trust in her judgement
* Turning to alcohol or tranquilizers to dull the torment.

The unfortunate thing is many of the victims try to deal with the trauma on their own. Crisis centers and counseling groups are available to help victims go through a very difficult period. They have the experience and empathy to help provide needed support. No one wants to be raped. It is not the victims fault. Society has a long way to go to recognize this. Victims need our support. But only for the grace of god, anyone of us could have been the victim. A victim has the right to be angry. But don't just be angry, do something about it.

Steps to making a recovery:

Share your feelings - a trusted friend or counselor can help in the recovery period.

Rape Crises Centers - I have found these people to be particularly dedicated. They have the experience and knowledge to help the victim in the recovery process.

They are familiar with the legal process, counseling and will support whatever decision the woman chooses.

Taking care of yourself:

a. Recognize you are a survivor and are important to others around you i.e. family, friends, children etc.

b. Realize it wasn't your fault

c. Pamper yourself physically and psychologically

d. Relaxation tapes might be useful

Regaining control:

a. Join a self defense class

b. Look into ways of being and feeling safer. Prevention and awareness training to learn how to be more alert.

c. Look people in the eye: a strong sign of confidence.

To recover, you must take the first step. Don't let one creep stop you from reaching your goals or aspirations.

QUESTION: HOW MIGHT BEING INVOLVED IN EXERCISE HELP TO REDUCE THE CHANCE OF BEING A VICTIM?

Strong evidence suggests that a good exercise program (almost any type), goes a long way to improve a person's view of herself. Psychiatrists and psychologists are even prescribing exercise to combat depression. Anyone involved in exercise can tell of the "highs" achieved after a good workout. All that is needed is about 30 minutes of exercise 3 times a week. It is thought that exercise stimulates the release of chemicals that produce a good feeling. Over the long-term these feelings are reflected in the person's feelings about herself. Feeling stronger, more vibrant, and more fit appears to increase a person's confidence level. This added confidence is reflected in the person's walk, posture and attitude. This will also be important in telling a potential attacker "don't mess with me."

QUESTION: HOW DO YOU PICK AN ACTIVITY OR SPORT?

You might have to try several activities before one suits your fancy. There are so many to pick from, everyone should be able to find one they like. Are you interested in an aerobic type or anaerobic type? Do you find pleasure in group exercise or individual exercise? Do you like competitive or non competitive sports? A lot depends on your personality, time and location. There are numerous sports magazines and the library to give you an idea of what you might like to try. Start with any activity, as long as you start. You can always switch if you find it is not for you. Check with a doctor if you are over 35, smoke, are overweight or have not exercised in a long time. Moderation is the key to success.

THE DATING GAME

GENERAL INFORMATION

No other activity carries with it the risk of rape more than dating. ***It accounts for a whopping 50% of the rape statistics.*** Studies have shown the victim is predominantly in the 15 to 24 year old range. As we might expect, date rape most frequently occurs on weekends between 10 p.m. and 2 a.m. There is less chance that a weapon is used under these circumstances. We see greater use of verbal threat and pure physical force to intimidate and overpower the victim. Date rapes tend to last longer, often stretching over 4 hours. While it is unlikely that the risk of rape can be totally eliminated from a dating situation, there are a number of steps that can be taken to substantially reduce the risk.

Colleges are an attraction for rapists. The environment is very conducive for rapists to operate and locate unsuspecting victims with the congenial nature of campus life, sometimes even a party-like atmosphere exists, and makes it easy to meet new people. Rapists will frequent school hangouts and drop in on parties that are often easy to attend. Colleges are becoming more concerned about the incidence of rape on campus.

Some college campuses are offering rape prevention information during their orientation program. To a large degree, information about rape on campus is suppressed to avoid giving the school a bad reputation. What the administration doesn't realize is that it happens at the best and the worst schools. Keeping the information quiet only helps the rapist. Only through education of the college community will the problem best be dealt with.

DATING TIPS

* Try grouping on the first date. Going out alone with a stranger presents a high risk situation. This is regard less of how "nice" someone appears. Remember you "can't judge a book by its cover," either.

* Care should be taken about isolating yourself with a new friend. After taking the time to group date, you later go off in his car alone, return to his apartment or bring him into yours. Remember, there are two pre requisites for rape: isolation and uninterrupted time.

* Set limits on your companion so he will know how far you are prepared to go. Make sure your body language is saying the same thing you are saying. Commonly misread body language is one of the rapist's excuses. Many young males, less experienced in a dating situation, are not able to clearly read these signals. Be sure to communicate intentions to your date early enough so that there will be no misunderstanding.

* Bar hopping is like playing Russian roulette. That is just asking for trouble.

* Liquor or drugs when dating lowers resistance and alertness. This makes you more vulnerable. Alcohol and drugs are usually associated with the rapist. About 20% of the time it has been found that the victim was under the influence. Many states have passed laws to protect females. Any sexual act committed on a female, while under the influence of alcohol, will be considered rape.

* While taking a ride from or offering a ride to a new friend might appear like the neighborly thing to do, it places you in unnecessary danger. College students are especially vulnerable. Often, limited funds make the temptation of sharing rides a frequent reality. Postings in college dorms such as "wanted-student to share expense to..." are invitations to danger. Many college girls have disappeared on trips like these.

* Be wary of a companion who constantly tries to control all the dating activities and must always get his own way. Often this is transferred to an intimate situation as well. He does not take "no" for an answer.

QUESTION: WHAT DO YOU DO IF YOU ARE A VICTIM OF RAPE OR SEXUAL ASSAULT?

While each of us would dread the prospect of ever being a rape victim, there is always that possibility that you or someone close to you might be one. Rape and sexual assault are extremely traumatic experiences. After a rape, depression and low self esteem can occur. Support is needed. Every effort must be made to return the victim's life to its normal course. It will not be easy. The effort will be made easier by the sympathetic help of family, friends and loved ones. They will help considerably in the recovery. However, professional help will also be important. Crisis centers, psychologists and mental health workers have experience and can be of invaluable assistance to the victim. Don't ignore professional help. The victim went through a terrible experience that she was unable to avoid. She just happened to be in the wrong place at the wrong time.

REMEMBER: IT WAS NOT HER FAULT.
NOBODY WANTS TO BE RAPED.

CHECKLIST FOR VICTIMS

* Call police immediately. Request a female officer if you wish.
* Don't wash or douche.
* Have a medical exam and an internal gynecological exam as soon as possible.
* Have any bruises, cuts or marks recorded at time of examination.
* Submit any personal clothing that was torn or damaged, especially undergarments (for semen analysis) etc. A recent discovery now makes it possible to match a rapist's hair, blood or sperm with near certainty. It matches the DNA of the suspect with a sample obtained from the victim. The process takes about one week and costs between $500 - $800. Hopefully, in the future, both the time and cost factors will be reduced.
* Show marks or bruises to a friend or relative for further corroboration.
* As soon as you are calm, write down everything you can

remember about the incident. (Review suspect ID chart)

* Be sure to get investigating officer's card so you can contact him/her in the future if need be.
* It is important to be tested for VD and pregnancy at some point. Check with doctor. Usually about 6 weeks.
* Seek professional help. Don't try to deal with this alone. It is usually too much for one person. Check with a rape crisis center. They will understand what you have experienced and provide you with the help and support you need.

QUESTION: SHOULD I PRESS CHARGES?

A tough question arises as to whether or not to go through the ordeal of pressing charges. This usually exposes the victim to further pain and stress. Be prepared for tough going. However, if charges are not pressed, the rapist will return to society, undoubtedly, to rape again. As we now recognize, rapists are sick and are unable to prevent themselves from repeating the crime. The choice is yours to make. At times it might appear that the victim is on trial. Many states require that a woman put up a fight against an assailant in order to prove rape occurred. Yet, this is contrary to advice by experts that when threatened with a weapon, it is best not to resist. Also, what about a situation where another family member is threatened with harm if the victim does not comply? Without injuries, the defense will generally try to prove the victim was actually a willing partner. So the chances of winning are not always as simple as what they might appear to be. Rape is the only crime where the victim is often forced to prove her innocence.

QUESTION: WHAT MIGHT I BE ASKED WHILE TESTIFYING IN COURT?

Certain specific areas will almost always be included in the questions asked during the proceedings.

* Discussion about the events leading up to the event; where and when you met or came in contact with the rapist. You will be asked about what you were doing and what was said, if anything.

* Questions about the physical part of the rape and what happened. Descriptions of the rapist, the circumstances and the surroundings.

* Questions pertaining to what you did after the incident. When did you report it? What documentation do you have? (Police reports, medical records and witnesses will all play important parts in this phase of questions.)

IDENTIFYING A SUSPECTED ASSAULTER

QUESTION: HOW CAN I HELP THE POLICE CATCH SOMEONE WHO HAS ATTACKED OR THREATENED ME?

One of the best ways to help the police is by giving as comprehensive a description as possible. The following identification poster will help make you aware of what to watch for in making a good I.D.

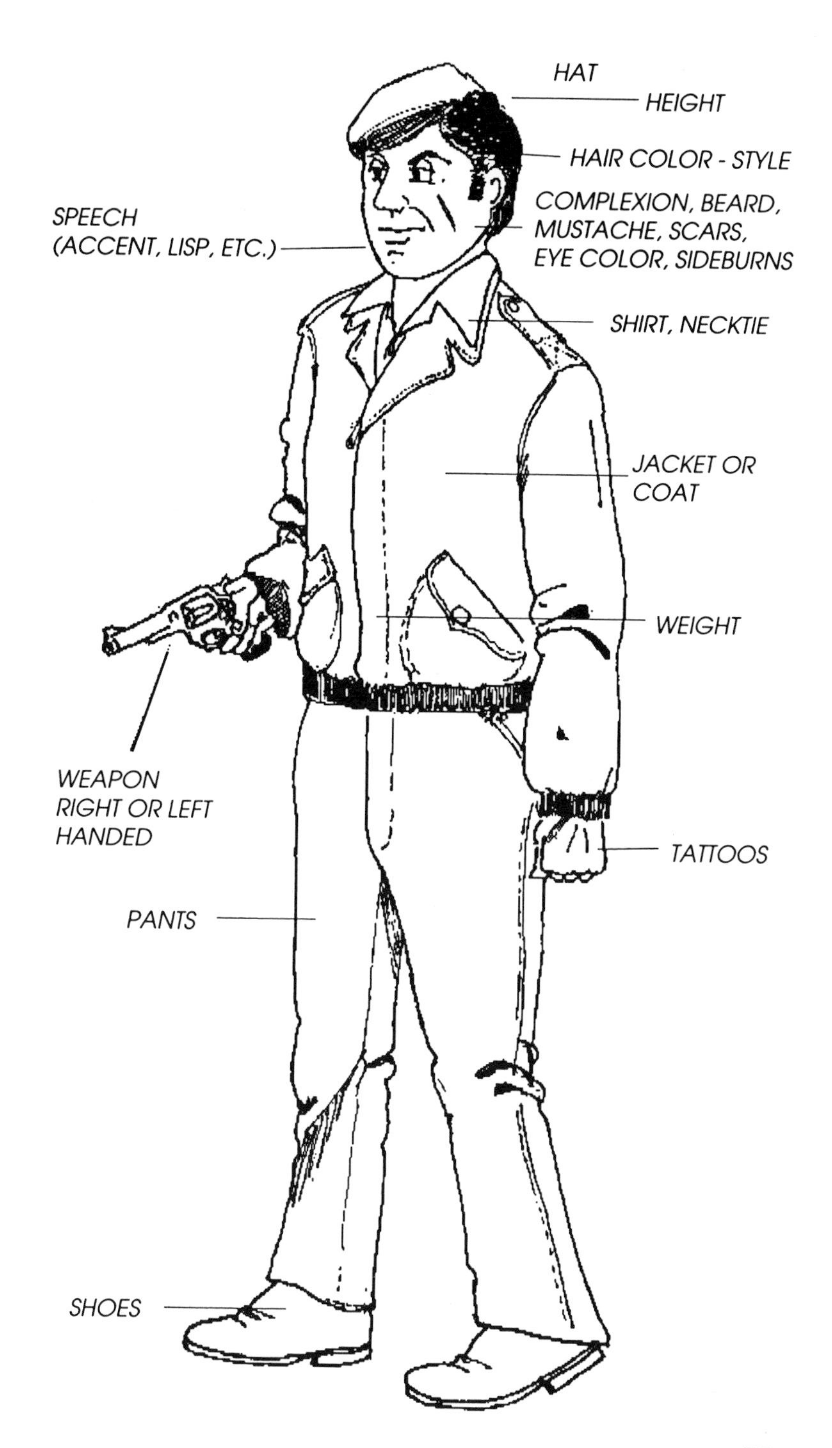
HAT
HEIGHT
HAIR COLOR - STYLE
SPEECH
(ACCENT, LISP, ETC.)
COMPLEXION, BEARD,
MUSTACHE, SCARS,
EYE COLOR, SIDEBURNS
SHIRT, NECKTIE
JACKET OR
COAT
WEIGHT
WEAPON
RIGHT OR LEFT
HANDED
TATTOOS
PANTS
SHOES

PROTECTING OUR CHILDREN

Recently, more and more information has been surfacing and it appears that many young girls under age 10 have bee subjected to rape and sexual abuse. However, you can recognize how difficult it is to get accurate information. Most of this has come to the surface after interviewing women in their late teens and early twenties. While they could not reveal this secret when they were younger, they are now able to speak about it. According to one study, it appears that as many as one in eight preteen girls have been sexually abused; and usually the abuser is a family member or close family "friend." Early information seems to indicate this to be true in about 90% of the cases. For the most part, this abuse goes unreported. When reported, little is done. How could a three or five year old report something like this? Children are often confused and do not know what to do or with whom to speak.

QUESTION: WHAT CAN I TELL MY CHILD?

There are a number of things a parent can tell a child.

1. It's your body; no adult should be touching you when you don't want them to.

2. If you feel that something wrong is being done by an adult, then you are probably right.

3. Tell someone. Tell Mom, Dad, brother, sister, relative, friend, teacher or clergyman until something is done about it, so it won't happen again.

4. Go through the procedure for answering the phone and what to say when they are home alone. Never say, "I am home alone." They might say, "My mother or father can't come to the phone right now, but if you leave your name and number, I will have her call you back shortly."

5. Warn children about opening the door to anyone other than immediate family members. Remember, most cases of child abuse do occur by persons known to the child.

QUESTION: WHAT SIGNALS MIGHT INDICATE MY CHILD IS BEING SEXUALLY ABUSED?

Children are not likely to discuss sexual abuse. Many don't know who to talk with or what to say. A majority of children are afraid to discuss it. However, carrying such a burden with them often appears as changes in attitudes or behavior. As parents, we must be alert to possible signals. Some of these might be:

* Changes in behavior such as eating habits, loss of sleep, more aggressive and disruptive, or withdrawing from regular activity.

* Changes in friendships and relationships.

* Marks or irritations on the genitals and/or anal area.

* Difficulty in concentration. Change in school performance.

* An unexplainable fear or dislike for an adult, whether it be a close family friend or relative.

While any one or more of these symptoms might occur for other reasons, this might give you a clue to discussing it with your child. Most states have child abuse hotline numbers if you need further help or suspect that your child is being sexually abused.

TRAVELING, VACATIONING
&
PUBLIC TRANSPORTATION

QUESTION: WHAT TIPS CAN YOU GIVE SOMEONE WHO TRAVELS ALONE?

There are a number of precautions to take to greatly reduce the risk of being victimized when traveling.

* Travel with friends whenever possible.

* Avoid public restrooms when possible. When absolutely necessary to use them, be on your guard and be as quick as possible. Don't totally believe in the safety of a locked door.

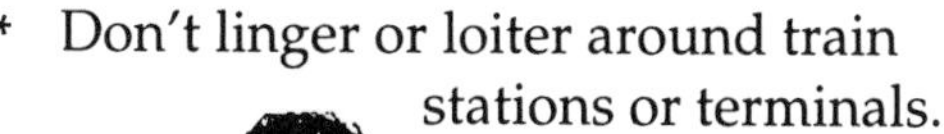

* Don't linger or loiter around train stations or terminals. Leave with the crowd.

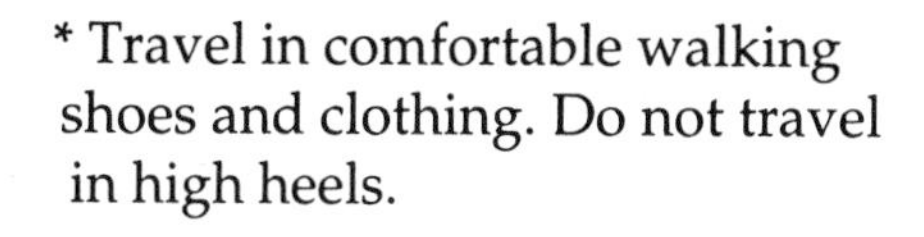

* Travel in comfortable walking shoes and clothing. Do not travel in high heels.

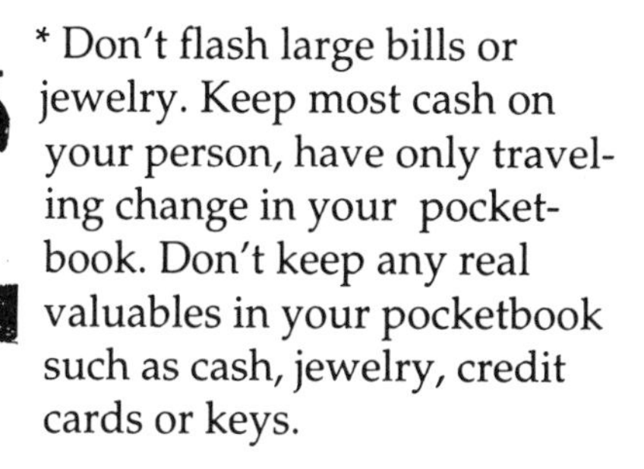

* Don't flash large bills or jewelry. Keep most cash on your person, have only traveling change in your pocketbook. Don't keep any real valuables in your pocketbook such as cash, jewelry, credit cards or keys.

* Don't travel overloaded with cases or bags.

* Walk directly and with purpose. Be confident, and be alert.

* Do not respond to catcalls, whistles or remarks; this encourages the person or persons doing it.

* Plan your route in advance. Avoid shortcuts, alleys, dark or deserted places. Use well-lit streets.

* When coming home late at night on a regular basis, vary your route.

* When leaving work late, leave with a group; don't be the last one.

* Don't take lifts from strangers.

* Don't hitchhike.

* Be alert after getting off a bus or train that no one is following you.

* Minimize conversation on public phones. You tend to be unaware of what is happening around you.

* Stay near ticket or toll booths until train arrives. Stay near conductor or driver. Sometimes it is better to stand and be safe.

* Don't travel alone if you are ill, under the influence of medicine, alcohol or drugs. Being followed: go to nearest public place (store, restaurant etc.) and have someone call police.

* Being followed: go to nearest public place (store, restaurant etc.) and have someone call police.

QUESTION: WHAT PRECAUTIONS CAN I TAKE WHEN PLANNING A TRIP OR VACATION?

Vacationers have always been a target of a variety of criminal types. Numerous scams and techniques are used on the unwary traveler. One of the reasons vacationers are targeted is because they are loaded with cash, credit cards, jewelry and clothing. In addition, the vacationer's "on vacation" attitude or mindset makes them ripe for the picking. The vacationer wants to relax and get away from the troubles and headaches of work, family, dangers of the city etc. Also, the low key, relaxing environment of hotels, motels, resorts and vacation areas doesn't lend itself to keeping alert. It is necessary to follow the same rules for alertness as described in the Chapter on Resistance. Once you are in a public place, any public place, on vacation or not, you must be alert to potential danger. Some additional facts that might be useful:

* If you plan on leaving the country, check with the U.S. Department of State about areas that should be avoided. They have a list of places that seem to present real danger to American citizens. Your travel agent might not be aware of this information. You know the country, island or resort will do all in its power to conceal this information.

* Have a trusted friend, neighbor or relative keep an eye on your home or apartment. See the chapter on the home for additional security tips.

* Don't put your home address on your luggage labels. Instead, put the travel agents office, your business or a friends address. Criminals have been known to wait at bus or plane terminal luggage areas to get the address of the people who are going away from home.

* Motels and hotels have recently been targeted by the media and insurance companies as places with little or no security. Strangers have been given keys to rooms upon request at the front desk. So don't leave valuables in your room. Check them at the desk or take them with you. Travelers checks and credit cards are probably better than cash. Keep the check numbers in a different spot in case they are stolen. Keep a phone number to the credit card company in the event they are stolen.

* Keep your money and credit cards in several places. Also, you might carry a "dummy" wallet with a few bills and outdated credited cards which can be given to a thief on demand. A mugging generally takes 20 seconds or less, the thief will not take time to check the dates on the cards. Remember, he who laughs last, laughs best. Can you imagine the expression on the thief's face when he realizes the outdated cards are useless.

* Don't ever resist giving your money, your car or your valuables to an armed thief when personal safety is in question.

* Keep some small change handy for tips or phone calls.

* Don't travel so overloaded with luggage as to make you look vulnerable. You could pre-ship anything greater than you can carry by yourself or re-evaluate whether you really need all that junk. This "overloaded" look attracts criminals.

THE CAR

QUESTION: WHAT SAFETY TIPS CAN YOU GIVE SOMEONE WHO TRAVELS BY CAR?

Next to one's home, the car was thought to offer a measure of safety from the violence that was occurring on the street. This myth has been shattered by the wave of carjacking cases which have spread across the country. The public is beginning to recognize that safety is a full time job. This new wave of crime has shaken the public's confidence to its' roots.

In an effort to cut down on this crimewave, carjacking has been made a federal crime with serious penalties. However, it hasn't discouraged all criminals from this practice. One reason might be how easy a carjacking is to pull off. The crime offers the criminal a chance of a multiple payoff which could include a car, money and/or valuables. This is particularly lucrative during the holiday shopping season.

Recent riots have shown how vulnerable one could be in the "safety" of their own car. There are some key points to keep in mind. A moving car offers a greater measure of protection than one stopped at a light or a stop sign or moving slowly in heavy traffic. A moving car can be a lethal weapon. Try to prevent from being boxed in. At a light or stop sign, always leave room enough to move ahead or even around the car in front of you. A minimum of one car length should be sufficient.

Maintain the same level of alertness while driving as you would walking in the street, especially when you stop or slow down. One should be in Color Code Yellow as explained in the chapter on resistance. Each and every time the car stops or slows down, it is important to be aware of what is going on around you. Use your rear view and side mirrors to help in the process. Don't get too engrossed in distractions such as daydreaming, the radio or a tapedeck.

A number of effective measures can be taken in the daily use of the automobile.

* Service car regularly. Breakdowns always seem to happen at the worst time and place. Don't use the excuse, "I was too busy to have it serviced." Are you too busy to break down? Learn to check gas, tires, battery, water and oil. Do it regularly.

* Carry a "GET HELP" sign to be put in your car window in case of a road side emergency.

* Don't allow anyone to give you a lift or come into your car. Have them get help for you.

* Don't park your car where it will be isolated when you return. Be sure the area will be well lit if you return after dark.

* Don't leave keys with parking attendant. Copies can be made.

* Have someone walk you to your car whenever possible.

* Always shut off and lock your car when leaving, even if for only a minute.

* Never leave the car running.

* Keep a can of tire inflator in the car. It might help you get to the nearest gas station in an emergency.

* Never go home if you think you are being followed. Go to police or fire station. Other choices might be a 24 hour gas station or fast food restaurant. Do not leave your car; instead start blowing your horn and attract attention.

* You are generally safer in a locked car than trying to leave it. Blow your horn. If necessary, you can use you car as a weapon. Run down your attacker.

* Keep doors locked when traveling. Windows should never be opened more than an inch or two: not enough for a hand to get in.

* Underground garages can be treacherous. Avoid them when possible. Park near entrance or exit. Otherwise, have someone escort you. If alone, enter when you see a group enter or leave. Do not linger there.

* Don't keep your house keys on your car key ring. The crook might have dinner at your house after robbing your car.

* Don't store the vehicle registration in your car, your driver's license or other documents with names and addresses.

* Don't have a pocketbook on the seat. Cover valuables inside the car or, even better, put them in the trunk of your car. This will help deter the criminal from smashing your window when you stop at a light to steal your package or bag.

* Always keep your car in drive when you stop at a light or stop sign.

* If someone approaches your car with a stick, pipe or knife, don't hesitate to drive off.

* If someone approaches with a gun, let him have your car. The experts agree, you can't outrun a bullet. Do anything short of antagonizing the person to avoid being taken along. Falling in the street faking a heart attack might be just the right distraction. There is a documented case where a women used the tactic to startle the criminal and frighten him off a criminal.

* Rest areas are often hangouts for undesirables looking for an easy target. Watch your kids as well.

* In my opinion, one of the best deterrents to a successful auto theft is the delayed engine cut-off. More and more alarms are being ignored . A good car thief can inactivate most car alarms. However, once the theft is made and the thief is escaping, the automatic delayed shut-off catches him unaware and unprepared. The sudden surprise will frighten off all but the most determined criminals.

QUESTION: WHAT'S THE SAFEST WAY TO CHECK OUT MY CAR BEFORE ENTERING?

* Begin checking at a distance. Look underneath. Check out any nearby vehicles or places where someone could hide or jump out from.

* Have keys in hand before you approach car.

* Check both rear and front seat before entering. Keep looking around and have your eyes open.

* Use the Color Code System (explained in Chapter on Resistance) while approaching or operating your vehicle.

QUESTION: IS YOUR CAR A TARGET FOR A BREAK IN OR CAR THIEF?

Recent evidence has come to light that thieves in search of drugs are singling out certain cars. They are attracted to "muscle" cars, cars or vans that sport rock and roll bumper stickers or other clues that the owner might be a user of marijuana or cocaine. It is also known that certain models are particularly attractive to the "chop shop" trade. Check with your insurance company, they can tell you which cars are primary targets of "chop shop" operators. You will probably find the insurance premiums for this "target" group are well above the average car.

HOME

OR

APARTMENT

Since a substantial number of ***rapes occur in the home or apartment, (about 50%)*** and in many cases the victim's dwelling, it is imperative that we look to increase security in this area.

QUESTION: WHAT STEPS CAN I TAKE AROUND MY HOME OR APARTMENT TO PREVENT UNWANTED INTRUSIONS?

Many positive steps can be taken to increase security around the home. But, first, let us consider how an attacker may enter. First, we have the break-in. Second, there are those that "con" their way in. Phoney deliveries, inspectors or "can I use your phone" type excuses often gain entry. Another common ploy is "my car broke down" or "my friend is injured, can I call an ambulance ?" In the first place, the door should never be opened to these people. You make the call if one has to be made. Finally, there are those we invite in because they are "friends, acquaintances or family." Date rape accounts for a very large proportion and these men usually get an invitation. More discretion is needed in this area, but we all recognize that this is the most difficult to prevent. What steps can be taken for improved home security?

* Use of solid wood or metal doors and dead bolt locks. A door is only as good as the lock and vice versa. Lock the door each time you enter and leave if only for a minute or two. Instruct children to do the same. Doors are the burglar's first choice of entry.

* Peepholes in doors enable you to see who is outside without opening the door. Doorchains are of little value because they are held with small screws which can easily be ripped out.

* Windows with adequate locks. They are the burglar's next choice of entry after doors. Jalousie type windows are easy to get into, so avoid them.

* Adequate lighting. Rapist and burglars like to come in by surprise. Lighting discourages this. Exterior light sensors (turn on at first signs of darkness), infra-red detectors and timers are all readily available. Indoor timers can turn on lights, radios etc.: when turned on at different timed intervals, they give the impression people are at home.

* Alarm Systems. Modern electronics have provided a great variety of security devices, many reasonably priced. Obviously the more you spend, the more sophisticated a system you can install. Devices range from foiled windows, infra-red detectors, motion detectors, to sound sensors and electric eyes. Panic buttons are useful at main entrances and near beds. An alarm system should be equipped with a back-up battery in the event of a power failure, accidental or intentional. Discuss what you want with a reputable installer because they will help you set up the best system that you can afford.

* Some tips on selecting a security specialist will be provided in this section.

* Single women living alone should not put their first name on the mailbox. Last name and first initial only i.e., P. Jones.

* Sliding doors can provide easy access. They can be lifted up out of the track. Find out how to prevent this.

* Have keys handy when you come home. Don't leave extra key hidden under mat or above door. The experts know where to look for hidden keys.

* Fire escapes offer easy entry, regardless of how high up you live. Keep those windows locked at all times.

* Have curtains closed in the evening.

* Bars on windows and doors are good at keeping intruders out. However, they have been known to keep people in during fire emergencies as well. Care must be given to quick escapes.

* Screen doors offer no security against even the most amateur of criminals.

* A dog around the house or apartment offers some advance warning. Also, it will discourage some perpetrators.

Apartment buildings could implement a number of steps to increase security such as:

a. Doorman or roving security; especially utilized at peak crime hours.

b. Buzz-in system with key access. Use of intercom to know who is downstairs and wants entry.

c. Closed circuit cameras.

d. Tenant Patrols. Volunteers will take turns during peak crime hours.

e. Ask local police department to evaluate building for suggestions on how to improve security. No precautions are fool proof and can totally eliminate the threat of a determined rapist or criminal. So, no matter how many safety measures are implemented, it is still up to the individual to maintain mental alertness.

QUESTION: WHAT SHOULD I KNOW ABOUT PURCHASING A BURGLAR ALARM SYSTEM?

ABOUT THE COMPANY

* Check with town/county/city if they require licensing for this type of business. Then check each company to see if it is licensed. Recommendations from friends who have had a system put in are helpful.

* Local company or not. Usually local companies are easier to get service and help. How long have they been in business? This is important. Get a list of customers in the area they have done work for and call a few.

* Check with local Consumer Affairs Office, the Better Business Bureau, or the Chamber of Commerce to see if complaints have been lodged against company. If no complaints are listed, this does not necessarily mean the company has none, but at least they are not flagrant about it.

* Do they offer 24 hour service? Do they give a guarantee or warranty? Do they offer a maintenance contract?

ABOUT THE SYSTEM

* Does the system have both an electrical hook up and back up battery? This protects against cut wires and blackouts and also prevents systems from going off accidentally during electrical failure.

* If the system is activated, will it automatically reset itself after a prescribed period of time? (15-20 minutes). Also, does the system have an outer/inner perimeter or both? Outer perimeter would include foiled windows, or shock sensors on windows. Wired doors are also part of this outer defense. Interior could include pressure sensors under mats or carpet, electric eyes, infra-red sensors, and motion detectors.

* Is the system locally activating an alarm or bell? Does it dial the police or private security?

* Is the system approved by Underwriter's Laboratories?

* Does the system include panic buttons? They are essential parts of an alarm system. One should be located near the front door, and one near the bed in the bedroom.

There are some systems being sold through hardware and home improvement centers. They are usually much cheaper than a professional set up. Some of them might do the trick for what your situation requires. However, look into them very carefully before investing. Remember an inexpensive system is no bargain if it doesn't work.

RESISTANCE

PASSIVE RESISTANCE

QUESTION: WHAT IS PASSIVE RESISTANCE?

Passive resistance is a technique of non violent, non-compliance that will usually confuse the rapist, but not anger him. Passive resistance is especially effective when the rapist tries to remove the victim from a public place (shopping center, public transportation, parking lot, etc). Its purpose is to buy time, attract attention, and confuse, but not antagonize the attacker. The rapist will be caught off guard in a situation he did not expect or easily deal with. It is likely he will depart as his plan begins to fall apart. Passive resistance is more acceptable to personality types not capable of open defiance. Some examples of passive resistance might include:

* Falling limp to the ground or fainting.

* Feigning a sprained ankle as he tries to drag you along.

* Pretending to have chest or abdomial pains, screaming in pain, be a possible heart attack victim.

* Vomiting by carefully putting fingers down your throat when rapist can not see.

Use your imagination, what other types of passive techniques can you think of? Bear in mind you must be convincing. Practice these with a friend to develop them to their best. Be aware that these techniques of resistance are best suited for public places where help is readily available. Once isolated, these techniques could backfire on you. The rapist is not under pressure to figure out how to deal with these circumstances and will probably inflict bodily injury to get your compliance. He does not care at this point that you scream in pain. Another passive technique that is a possibility, but will take a special person to accomplish, is that of diffusing the rapist's anger. Try to distract the rapist from his plan by talking to him as a person. Calm him down and let him view you as a person as well. "Fix the son of a bitch a steak if necessary," says psychiatrist Emilee Wilson. This technique will be attempted only after you are isolated and it boils down to trying this or active resistance. If this fails, you can always resort to active resistance anyway.

AN ESSENTIAL PART OF RESISTANCE BEGINS IN THE MIND AND IT STARTS WITH MENTAL ALERTNESS.

QUESTION: HOW ALERT MUST I BE?

Alertness is the key to preventive safety. Obviously, there are times when we are not very alert, but we don't have to be. I am often asked "How attentive do I have to be?" There are a number of considerations that come to mind. Normally, when out of your home, it is suggested that you function in Color Code Yellow. However, here again, we can learn much from watching animal behavior. Why do you think zebra, giraffe and other animals hang out in groups? There are more eyes, noses and ears that are working to detect danger. When in a group, your attention doesn't have to be at the same level of alertness that you need when you are alone. Also, the surroundings will determine the need to be more or less attentive. Take these factors into account and always **Trust Your Instincts**. It is always wiser to error on the side of safety.

Being mentally alert is probably one of the most important steps a woman can take to reduce being at risk on the street. One of the ways to accomplish this is a program developed by Jeff Cooper, a combat shooting instructor, for law enforcement personnel. I have made some modifications so that it can be used by women. The program establishes a color code to signify a particular state of mental alertness. To be mentally alert is not easy. It is almost a full time job at first, but eventually it becomes the way you function. However, you must work at it and train your mind.

COLOR CODE WHITE - This is the lowest level of mental alertness. You are totally unaware of what is going on around you. Sleep walking might be the closest thing to it. It appears some people go through life this way. This is the group that most crime victims are selected from. This is part of the "victim mentality." This is also the most dangerous level to be in when out in the street. Intoxication, whether by alcohol or drugs, places the person in this level. To make matters worse, even will power is diminished. Under these circumstances many of the rape victims do not even report the crime because they don't even realize what has happened.

COLOR CODE YELLOW- You are now aware of your surroundings. This level is often referred to as "scanning." Information from different stimuli is being brought in and evaluated. You are alert to what is going on around you, yet you are comfortable and not on edge. This is the level of mental alertness that should exist once you leave the safety of your home.

COLOR CODE ORANGE - Let your senses guide you into this level of alertness. TRUST YOUR INSTINCTS. Certain cues or signals will warn you of a possible threat or risk that might appear, maybe foot steps behind you, a shadow coming close or even a car following you. You begin to evaluate the danger as to its seriousness. This will lead into Color Code Red.

COLOR CODE RED - A plan of action has been formulated and is in the process of being implemented. It is at this point that you can still avoid a major confrontation i.e. you pull into your driveway and spot someone or something in the shadows. Be sure your door is locked and begin blowing your horn. Do not get out of the car and rush to the house. If necessary, back out of the driveway and get to the nearest phone and call police.

COLOR CODE BLACK - You are under assault. If you have not prepared yourself mentally, you will "panic" or "freeze." This offers little chance of escaping what will happen next. It is at this level that the benefits of martial arts training come in handy. It not only provides the physical means of fighting back, it also allows for clear thinking and plan formation. You will do whatever is necessary to be a survivor.

It is important to realize that it could be only a matter of a second or two before you go from condition white to black. It is necessary to start to play the game of mental alertness all the time. We must be careful not to become paranoid by operating in color code orange and red all the time, but to be in yellow where we are mentally alert. With practice it will become unconscious. In the beginning, you must force yourself to stay in code yellow. Remember this is one of the most important steps in the resistance process and reduces the risk of being a victim.

There is no universal prescription on how to react to a rape or sexual assault. And there is not one specific tactic or response that would work in every case. What might work for one woman might not work for another. What might frighten away one rapist could excite another. Time, place and personalities (both victim's and rapist's) are important considerations. It is difficult to know how you will react when confronted. It is a crisis situation and your response will be based most on conditioned responses. Your reaction and response are based on strong interacting factors of personality, temperament and training. It is important to remember that resistance begins in the mind. And that is why it is so essential that you try to keep a cool head. You will be better prepared to deal with it if advanced preparation is made. "The trained mind is prepared to act in any emergency," according to Capt. James Smith, a leading authority in women's rape prevention and author of Rape: Fight Back and Win! Understanding the dangers and the measures you can take are steps in the right direction. Knowing yourself is the first step.

1. Do you fear rape more than injury?

2. Do you fear injury more than being raped?

3. Are you more concerned about the risk to a friend or family member than of either being raped or injured?

4. Are you physically and mentally prepared to fight? Are you trained for it?

These are all important considerations. Knowing your capabilities and potential is a must.

QUESTION: WHAT FACTORS MUST BE CONSIDERED BEFORE IMPLEMENTING A COURSE OF ACTION?

The following list contains important considerations in determining a course of action.

* The rapist: how big? how angry? how many? Does he appear to be under the influence of alcohol or drugs?

* Does he have a weapon?

* Is there a chance of attracting attention?

* What are the chances of escape?

* Is help close by? Or am I totally isolated and on my own?

* Are environmental weapons handy?

It is important to remember, the best laid plans have been known to fail. So, it is important to have a back-up plan ready to go. Once these factors are considered, the choice of active or passive resistance must be made. There is also a third choice; that is complying with a rapist's demands and trying to get out of the situation alive and with as little damage as possible. With many women this is an unacceptable choice, but under certain circumstances it might be the only course of action recommended. Your ultimate objective is survival.

ACTIVE RESISTANCE

A recent study by the National Institute of Mental Health concluded that a woman who resists effectively is less likely to be raped than the woman who pleads, cries or otherwise complies. While this would include techniques of passive resistance, it also includes that of active resistance. According to Pauline Bart, co-author of Stopping Rape: Successful Survival Strategies, "women who had some self-defense training and fought back - even just by screaming and yelling - were about twice as likely to avoid rape. Pleading or trying to talk their way out of it didn't work." However, there are a number of things to consider if you are determined to offer active resistance in the event of an actual physical confrontation. Consideration should be given to:

* Does my personality allow me to fight off an attacker or will I be too easily intimidated? If you are dominant enough to fight back, that is a good start. However, if you feel that your personality type is too passive, then a strong effort and hard work might enable you to change it.

* Do I know enough about the rapist, since there are different personality types, to determine which would be the best type to offer active resistance against? This is often the most difficult question to answer. Active resistance, while effective against one type of rapist, might only cause a violent response from another type.

* Have I prepared several plans of action that can be quickly implemented under the right conditions? What does the situation dictate about my course of action? Obviously the same approach would not be taken in a movie theatre as in an isolated park or beach. You must learn how to play the different situations.

* How do I prepare myself for active resistance (war) because preparation is a must. Martial arts training will help develop the mental and physical tools that are needed to act under stress. Finding a good instructor is extremely important because he or she will guide you through all the necessary phases. The physical training will help you develop strength, balance, flexibility, coordination, stamina, speed and explosive power. Skill development would include learning the appropriate strikes and defenses. A leading instructor for the secret service, stressed that 3,000 - 5,000 repetitions of a technique are necessary before it can be done effectively and without thinking. So, practice is a crucial part of any training program. Many months of hard work are needed before these techniques can be relied upon under the stress of a street situation. Environmental training is important because most attacks will not be in a gym, but somewhere out in the street, wearing street clothes. Also, I think some mention should be made about the benefit of learning martial arts from a book or training tape. I don't believe someone can develop the necessary skills from either to be of any help. On the contrary, I believe a false sense of security develops that might cause more harm than good. Supervision and feedback is essential from an instructor who has proper training and teaching experience.

QUESTION: HOW EFFECTIVE IS YELLING OR SCREAMING?

Yelling or screaming can be very effective when help is close by. When used in conjunction with other forms of active resistance, it will help disorient your attacker, enabling other techniques to work more effectively. However, if you are alone and isolated, it is not suggested that you scream. It will probably enrage the rapist and encourage him to batter you. Several incidents occurring in the past have shown that yelling "FIRE" brings more desirable results.

QUESTION: DO YOU THINK MARTIAL ARTS TRAINING WOULD BE USEFUL IN AN ACTUAL CONFRONTATION WITH A MUGGER OR RAPIST?

I answer this question with over 30 years experience in the martial arts. Properly practiced and learned, martial arts training could be effective in a great number of encounters. No one defense has proven to be totally effective. While physical resistance, verbal resistance, noise-making devices, chemical agents (mace or OC), use of weapons, vomiting, urinating, defecating, pretext of pregnancy or venereal disease have all been successful in some instances, in other cases it could be worthless or dangerous. "To generalize the success of one or more instances to all rape situations is not only potentially dangerous to the victim, but is also irresponsible and unprofessional," according to agents Hazelwood and Harpold of the FBI Behavioral Science Unit. This is why I suggest that thought be given to a proper training program and time should not be a limiting factor. I am sure you wouldn't want the people who put your car together to have been in a hurry. According to the FBI agents, "potential victims have an excellent chance of surviving a rape confrontation if they are prepared in advance." However, the only thing worse than no training is a little training and no practice. So, I am not speaking about a short self-defense course that is quickly forgotten. I am talking of long term martial arts training. Not only will proper training build confidence, but it will increase awareness, allow you to think more clearly under stress, provide preplanned courses of action, and increase your strength, balance and coordination. In total, it will make you less of a "victim personality."

QUESTION: WHAT DO YOU THINK PROPER MARTIALS ARTS TRAINING SHOULD INCLUDE?

The following are key ingredients for a successful martial arts training program:

* The desire to learn (recognizing the need and the benefits) and the willingness to work hard at it.

* A good instructor is the key to a successful program. He must be knowledgeable, able to transmit the principles and concepts so that the student can understand them. While fluent English is not a must, he or she must be able to communicate the concepts in addition to demonstrating the mechanical motions of a technique.

* Quality Time - A minimum or 3-4 hours per week for at least 6 months is required to obtain the minimum amount of conditioning that will allow you to react in a situation without thinking. You have now developed a number of conditioned responses. Many people wait till the last minute and begin training. Then they want to learn in a hurry, but there are no shortcuts to training. Remember it has been found that 3,000-5,000 repetitions are necessary for an action to become subconscious. If you are not willing to make this time commitment, than martial arts training is not for you. It is not enough to react in a conscious way in the tranquil environment of a Martial Arts School. On the contrary, in the street it will often be a subconscious response under stress.

QUESTION: HOW DO I FIND A GOOD MARTIAL ARTS SCHOOL?

This is not always an easy job. The inexperienced can be misled by incredible claims and phoney propaganda. Below are some things to consider:

* Go in and watch a class. Pick up literature if available. Watch how the instructor teaches. Does he spend time explaining things to students or is everything done by imitation? Imitation training is very limited. It is important to understand the theory behind why techniques work. Information about anatomy and physiology, physics of balance and psychology of confrontation are important factors to be taught. Instructor's rank is not critical. The highest ranking is not necessarily the best.

* Speak with students about what they feel they have gotten out of training. Watch how skillful they are. Have they developed good balance and power? Do their movements look strong, smooth and powerful?

* Choose a school that offers both a traditional oriental martial arts philosophy and a practical approach to street self defense.

* Be wary about "the technique that works all the time." There are no such techniques. Nothing works 100% of the time.

* Avoid a school that trains strictly for tournament competition, or some of the Chinese arts that only perform fancy forms. You should see people working on two person drills and self defense techniques. Fancy is not usually the most practical.

* Watch out for the "Macho" school where they beat you up to train you for street confrontations.

* Avoid classes that are all female. You will not be attacked by a woman. You must train with men to beat men. Opponents of different sizes and strengths are needed to build skills and confidence.

* Make sure the techniques taught can be done in street clothes.

* Don't get sidetracked by fancy surroundings. It's nice to train in a spa-like atmosphere, but many good teachers teach in a Spartan setting.

* Learning a basic weapon that can be applied to the street can be beneficial. Arnis de Mano, a Philippine art, is a very practical type art. It will allow you to use anything you pick up as a weapon.

ENVIRONMENTAL WEAPONS

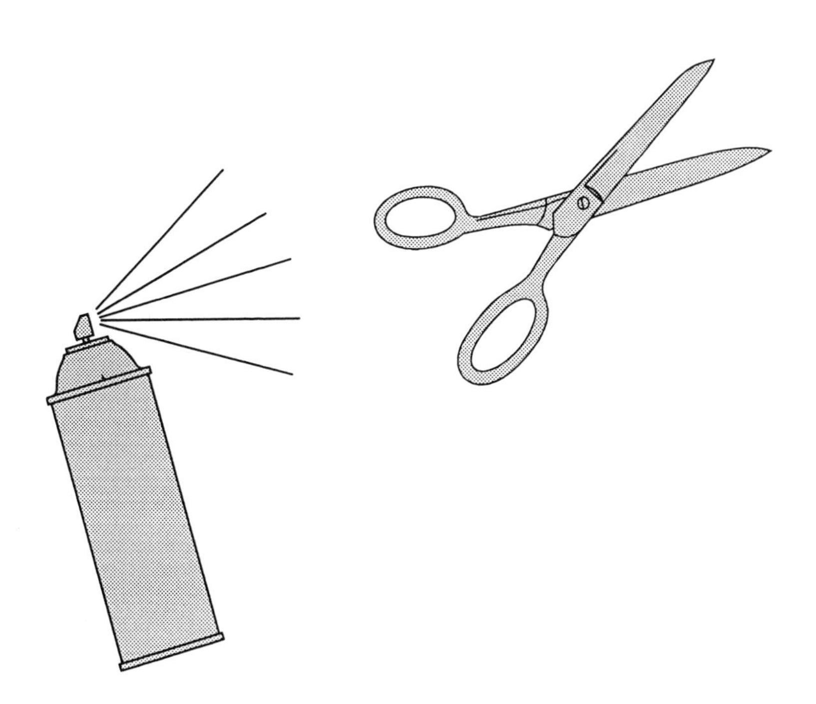

QUESTION: WHAT ARE ENVIRONMENTAL WEAPONS AND HOW ARE THEY USED?

Environmental weapons are objects and substances found commonly around that normally serve some utilitarian purpose other than being a weapon. However, when your life is threatened these commonly found materials can be turned into lethal weapons. Become familiar with the list that follows. Then begin to examine your surrounding for others at your disposal. No one knows for sure when or where they will be attacked, so it is important to be able to locate these environmental weapons quickly. These weapons might include:

KITCHEN - all sorts of kitchen utensils such as a knife, fork, spoon, pot or pan, bottle opener, etc.

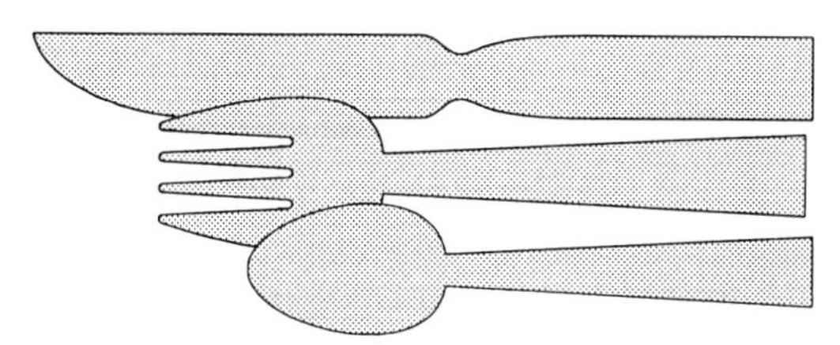

HOUSEHOLD ITEMS - scissors, ash tray, flashlight, toilet plunger, aerosol cans and spray cleaners or poisons, plate, powder, vacuum wand, lamp, telephone etc.

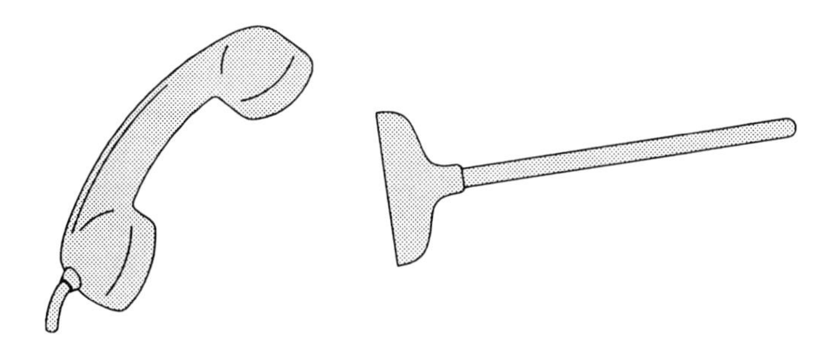

FIRE EXTINGUISHER - Captain Smith, a rape prevention expert, suggested the use of a fire extinguisher as both a chemical and a clubbing weapon. A light weight extinguisher kept in a car or at location around the house would be handy and effective if prior training in their use is given.

PERSONAL ITEMS - brush, comb, pen, pencil, nail file, hairspray, umbrella, or key, etc.

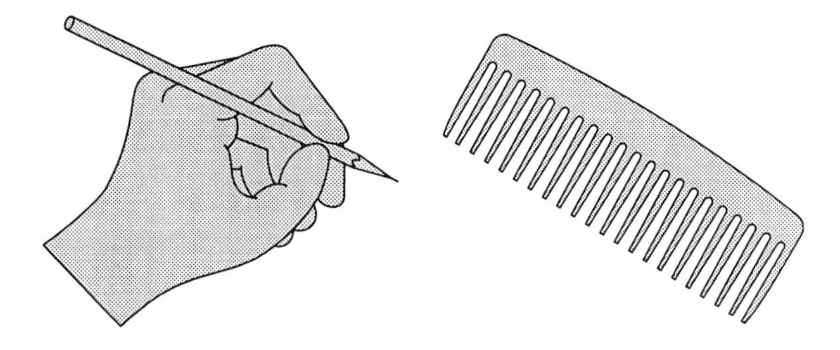

These are only a small number of what is available. In an emergency, you will be able to locate an environmental weapon quickly. Depending on the weapon used, attack one of the vulnerable parts of the body such as the eyes, throat, groin, etc. and escape. REMEMBER: Your main objective is to get away. The weapon provides you with an opportunity to stun or disable your attacker so escape can be accomplished.

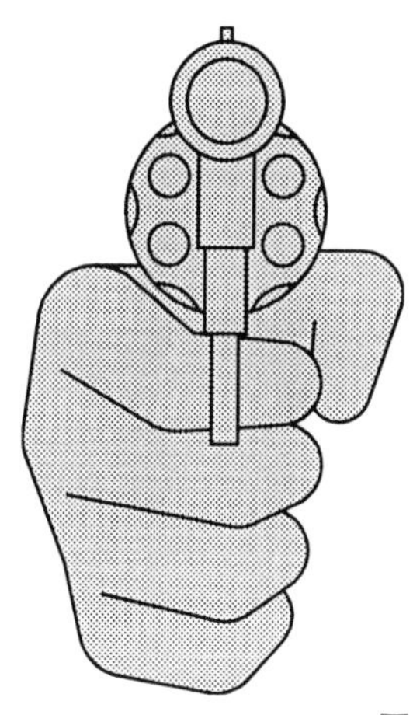

WHAT'S ON THE MARKET?

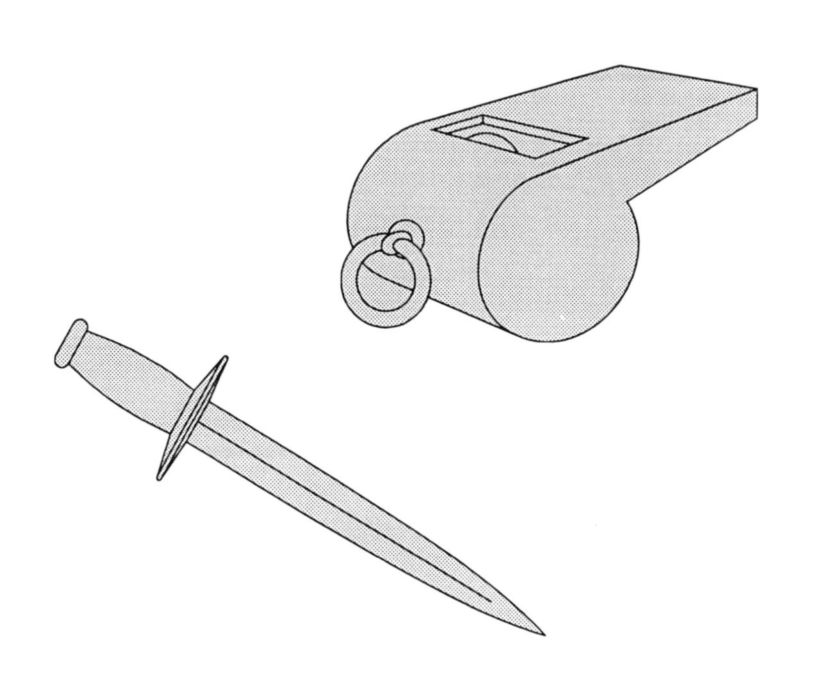

QUESTION: WHAT'S ON THE MARKET?

There are many different types of devices on the market designed to protect the potential victim. Since the market is so large, many weapons are available and many new ones appear all the time. However, I don't see any device that will totally guarantee your safety. Nothing will replace mental alertness and a cool head. We will next examine some of the devices available.

Noise devices come in a variety of sizes, shapes and loudness. The device is effective for two reasons. First, the criminal thinks it will attract attention and will be frightened off. In the second possibility, it actually attracts help. In the first situation, it didn't have to bring assistance, it only had to let the criminal think it would.

While experts agree that noise tends to frighten criminals, under certain circumstances, it could cause the armed criminal to shoot or injure his target. So, I stress again, it is important to know when and how to use any tool. Generally, when you are being directly threatened by an armed criminal, it is not the appropriate time to set off an alarm. This device is better used before the criminal approaches. If you are being physically assaulted by an unarmed attacker already, then activating the alarm, in most cases, can only be of help. If it is clear to the attacker that you are sufficiently isolated and no one is around to hear your alarm, the effectiveness of the device is all but eliminated. So don't view the device as an "end all" to your personal safety. Nothing will replace your best weapon; your mind, good judgement and common sense.

Several additional points should be considered for the effective use of this type of safety device. Is it handy? The best device is worthless unless you can get to it. Is it loud? We want to attract attention. It is unfortunate, but the public doesn't seem to react to sirens and alarms like they used to.

Another point, is the alarm trustworthy? Will it work when we need it to? Any product worth anything should have a one year guarantee. If a company gives a 90 day guarantee, they are not espousing confidence in their product. Why should you? Are the batteries charged? You should test your alarm periodically to be sure it works. Once activated, the alarm device should be difficult to turn off. Also, it should be sufficiently strong to resist being broken if thrown to the ground. This presents a major problem. To be completely shatter proof, the product would be priced totally out of range of what consumers might be able to afford. A solution might be attaching the device to your coat or clothing in some manner. Some can be looped through button holes or belts.

Since it is difficult or impossible to know the quality of a product from looking at it, under no circumstances would I purchase any of these products from a peddler off the street. Deal with the reputable store or mail order company. Some stores and companies now specialize in safety products. Through past experience, they will probably have selected products that are reliable and have good track record. The guarantee they offer is a sign of their confidence in the product. If your life is on the line, you want the best product for your money. More expensive doesn't necessarily mean better. Beware of the sales hype to sell the ultimate product. Remeber: your mind is the ultimate weapon; use it.

* Stun Guns. These produce a disabling electric charge. They are effective at close range. However, they must be applied to bare skin. In addition, they are now illegal in some areas.They can not be taken on aircraft and must be packed into luggage. Once again, the item might not be handy when needed. There is also a good chance that the stun gun might be taken away and used on the victim.

* Lethal Weapons. Some women carry concealed knives, guns, razors etc. for self defense. However, if not properly

trained, these weapons can be taken away and used on the victim. In addition , the woman might be subject to arrest for possession of a deadly weapon. Furthermore, actual use of these deadly weapons might result in arrest and / or lawsuits. They are generally not recommended.

The Truth About Chemical Agents

Since a good deal of effort is being made to promote chemical agents in the media and the public seems to be buying chemical sprays at record levels, I thought it would be worthwhile to discuss them. By listening to the sales pitch delivered by the companies, you would think that chemical sprays are going to solve the crime problem. After attending a number of seminars on chemical sprays, I understand where the average person could find it difficult to know which type, if any, is the best one to use. The following information will give you a better understanding of the types of sprays available to the public and what they are capable of doing.

* First, I want to discuss a number of criteria, I would like to see in a chemical agent. These should include:

* High reliability. It should work on every type of offender i.e. drug addict, drunk, psychotic, vicious animals etc. equally well. Both the dispenser and the product should be something we could place our trust in.

* The user should have no difficulty using the product even under stress.

* It should incapacitate the offender instantly. It should effect both sight and mobility.

* It should have no harmful or permanent side effects to the offender i.e. blindness, disfigurement or death. The possibility always exists that the sprayer might get some on them. Also, liability and justification is always a consequence to consider.

* It should be easily available or accessible at all times.

* Its effectiveness should not be diluted or neutralized by the weather or environment i.e. wind, humidity etc.

* The life expectancy of the product should be of reasonable length, I would think at least two years.

There are a number of types of chemical agents; however only two types have been marketed to the public for personal protection.

CN (Alphachloroacetaphenone)

Trade names - Mace, Curb, Freeze, Phaser

The most widely known CN product is Mace. Mace was originally designed to be sold to and used by law enforcement agencies. However, now it is being marketed to the public.

The law enforcement community found a number of short comings in the CN (Mace) product. First and foremost, its performance was inconsistent. Mace has not proven itself effective against drunks, drug addicts and psychotics. As these characteristics were common to many offenders, it was not a weapon the law enforcement community could count on.

Mace is an irritant and makes the eyes water. It usually takes 3-10 seconds to take effect. This is far too slowly if it is to be used as a self-defense tool. This allows a criminal too much time to use a weapon in order to get even. Not long ago, this is exactly the reason given by a murderer for killing a young female victim. Also, it has been found that Mace is not effective on drunks, drug addicts, psychotics and vicious animals. These are all important reasons for usage in the first place. In the past several years, the law enforcement community has been shifting to OC.

OC (Oleoresin Capsicum)

Trade names - Cap-Stun, BodyGuard, Pepper Mace, Defender, Defiance, Punch

OC acts instantaneously on contact with the mucous membranes of the eyes, nose and throat. It causes immediate dilation of the capillaries causing a swelling shut of the eye lids resulting in temporary blindness. In addition, it causes an inflammation of the respiratory passages making breathing difficult and severely limiting the intake of oxygen. OC is effective even against those individuals who feel no pain.

This is the newest and most effective of the chemical products on the market. It is a derivative of Cayenne Pepper and was first introduced to law enforcement in 1976. Since then, it has received extensive testing. By 1989 after three years of testing, the FBI Academy completed tests on over 3,000 subjects and adopted OC for use by its agents and special response teams. Because of its' ability to work on dogs and vicious animals, it is a favorite with the mailmen. It is considered to be a noxious substance, illegal in many states, so it is important to find out the laws in your community should you consider purchasing and carrying. Don't assume because it is sold in a store or flea market, it is legal to carry and use.

While the 1% solution is marketed to the public and 5% solution to police, it doesn't appear that the 5% is much more effective. In fact, as the concentrations go above 10%, they actually get less effective because of their inability to "atomize" or form droplets. Unlike CN and CS sprays, the OC not being a particulate, will not contaminate the area being sprayed.

OC itself, doesn't breakdown. However, because it is pressurized in an aerosol, over time there is leakage of the propellent gas, as in any aerosol, so it must be checked periodically for effectiveness. In any case, the spray should be tested outdoors in still air, so you will have an idea as to range and coverage.

The OC spray should not be used at distances closer than 2 feet. At this distance, the spray doesn't have a chance to "atomize" and form a mist. This is crucial to it taking effect rapidly. Also, because it is a mist, it doesn't carry well beyond 6-10 feet. Bear in mind, the effect of the spray will extend a foot or two beyond the visible spray in what is known as an invisible ball of Capsaicinoid. This is part of the 6-10 reach already mentioned. However, a lot would depend upon wind conditions. Care must be taken not to spray into a wind or breeze because the spray would be carried back into the sprayer. Together with the fact it can not be used under two feet, it does limit the spraying capacity. The key to successful use of any spray is twofold: proper training and correct application. Can this be properly pulled off under the stress of an assault? This is something to consider.

If we review the original requirements we established for our product, we find the OC meets more of our needs than does the CN (Mace) product. However, it is not perfect. The biggest concern is the mist spray application. As the mist is subject to wind and air movement, I am concerned that someone under stress won't always take this factor into account. Unfortunately, the mist is essential to the effectiveness of the gas agent. As far as it being an effective tool, I think it could be. However, training is essential. There are courses being offered to train the public in the use of the OC. I am very concerned about the public using the spray with little or no training. In addition, it is possible that the users could get a false sense of security and become careless or risky in their actions. Remember: the most important protection there is, is avoidance, prevention and awareness. The weapon should never be considered the first line of defense.

DIRECTORY

OF

QUALITY PRODUCTS,

Over the course of many years presenting dozens of seminars, I am frequently asked where or what device or product to buy. As I purchased items to test, I often found that the item was not up to the standard described by the manufacturer. Often I saw programs or heard advice that was marginal or downright dangerous if followed. Often the "expert" giving the information had limited experience or came from a particular point of view that contradicted information generally given by the law enforcement community. Often, the advice was centered around a particular product being sold i.e. spray gas, alarms, stun gun etc. The public is often unaware of what is good or bad. By the time they find out, it is often after the expense of a purchase. Even worse, they might find out when their life depends on the functioning of a crime prevention product. In my experience, I found the only thing worse than no program or safety advice is a bad one. Over time, I have come across many companies and individuals who looked to profit from the misfortune of others. When the time comes to rely on information or equipment in a life threatening situation, we want to know that we can count on it to work.

I decided that in future printings of the "Become Streetwise" book, I would add a section containing the names of companies, products and programs that I have found to be effective and purposeful. No fees are charged for a listing in this directory. In this way, I am not obligated to list any company or product. The companies and products are listed solely on their merit.

The following are a list of nonprofit and for profit companies which I feel offer a quality program and/or product. These individuals have shown concern about public safety. In addition, they offer a product or service that could be of value.

The nonprofit companies offer programs that would in the long run improve the quality of life. They focus on safety for young children or conflict resolution. Educators should seriously consider implementing these programs in their schools.

The products offered provide the individual with some increased measure of safety. Each item's value should be carefully considered before purchase.

New products and services are constantly being reviewed and might be included in future printings of the book.

Should you ever have difficulty with any company listed, I would be glad to hear from you. Any consumer problems could jeopardize a companies listing in this directory.

Stay safe.
Arthur Cohen

Arthur Cohen

President
Target Consultants Int'l

BIBLIOGRAPHY

A.C. "Personal Defense For Uncertain Times." Fight Back, Boulder Colorado, Omega Focus Series. May 1986: 4-7

Banks, William. "Choosing a Martial Art." Money, June 1986, 195-204.

Bates, Tom. "Protect Your Children." Fight Back, Boulder Colorado, Omega Focus Series. May 1986: 64-68.

Berglas, Steve. "Why Did This Happen to Me?" Psychology Today. February 1985: 23-25

Block, Richard J. Ph.D., Vane, Julia Ph.D., Barnes, Michael Ph.D., Kassinove, Howard Ph.D., Motta, Robert Ph.D A Study of Sex Offenders on Probation. New York: 1987

Borsch, Ron. "Chemical Agent Training." Justice System Training Associations's 11th National Training Seminar. June 1985.

Brody, Jane E. "Therapists Seek Cause of Child Molesting." New York Times. 13 January 1987: C12

Brittsan, Allison and Kelly, Vanessa. "Dealing With the Rarely Reported Acquaintence Rape," Nova Newsletter, February 1987: 6.

Brothers, Joyce Dr. "Date Rape". Daily News, 27, September 1987.

Campos, Michael. Rape Prevention. U.S.A., 1978.

Campos, Michael. A Fighting Chance: A Woman's Guide to Self-Defense. U.S., 1977.

Clede, Bill. "A Bouquet of Aerosol Sprays." Law and Order. September 1992:57-59

Clede, Bill. Police Nonlethal Force Manual. Harrisburg, PA: Stackpole Books, 1987.

Cohen, Arthur. Rape or Mugging: An Ounce of Prevention. New York: 1982.

Cohen, Arthur. "Rape And The Dating Game." Singles Says, June 1986: 8.

Early, Maureen. "Deterring the Rapist." Newsday. 26 January 1982: Part II. 8-10.

"Escaping Rape". Woman's Day. 19 August 1986, 84-87.

Everett, Pat. L, Everett, David. J. "The Complete Guide to Rape Prevention." Inside Kung Fu

Florida Office of the Attorney General. Help Stop Crime! Residential Burglary.

Florida Office of the Attorney General. Help Stop Crime! Sexual Assault.

Furby, Lita., Fischoff, Barach and Morgan, Marcia. Judged Effectiveness of Common Rape Prevention and Self-Defense Strategies.

Eugene Oregon: Eugene Research Institute, 1987. Judging the Risk of Rape.

Eugene Oregon: Eugene Research Institute, 1987. Rape Prevention and Self-Defense: At what price? Eugene Oregon: Eugene Research Institute, 1987.

Geberth, Vernon. "Stalkers." Law and Order Magazine. October 1992:138-143

Gross, Ken. "Target: BMW." The Roundel. December 1992:34-36

Grover, Jim. "Personal Security." Guns and Ammo. December 1992:40-41, 74-75

Hazelwood, Robert R. and Harpold, Joseph A. "Rape: The Dangers of Providing Confrontational Advice," FBI Law Enforcement Bulletin, June 1986: 1-5.

Hughes, Jean O'Gorman and Sandler, Bernice R. "Friends" Raping Friends Could It Happen to You?" Project on the Status and Education of Women. April 1987: 1-8.

Jacob, Don. Official Manual for Rape Prevention. Trinidad W.I., Purple Dragon Publication, 1986.

James, Anthony, "Environmental Weapons." Fight Back, Boulder Colorado, Omega Focus Series, May 1986: 26-29

Johnston, Gary Paul. "Rape Prevention For Men, Women and Children." Fight Back, Boulder Colorado, Omega Focus Series. May 1986: 76-79.

Leo, John. "Deadly Dilemma for Women." Time. 21 September 1, 1981: 75.

Long Island University Department of Criminal Justice and Security Administration. Women: Victims of Domestic Violence, Rape and Criminal Justice. ED. Roslyn Muraskin, New York, 1984.

Nassau County Police Department. ...in the next three minutes Ann Johnson will be the victim of RAPE.

Nassau County Police Department. Keep the Burglar in Check.

Nassau County Police Department. Robbery Almost the Worst Crime.

New York Borough Crisis Centers. Assisting Victims of Sexual Assault through Information, Referrals, Counseling & Advocacy.

New York Borough Crisis Centers. Guide to Medical Services Following Sexual Assault.

New York City Detective Bureau. Children!...Be Safe...Be Alert.

New York City Detective Bureau. WOMEN!...Beware...Be Aware.

New York City Police Department. A Child's Guide to Personal Safety.

Police Department City of New York Sex Crimes Analysis Unit. Protective Measures To Prevent Rape.

Rogers, Cindy Christian. "Fitness May Be a Woman's Best Defense." The Physician and Sports Medicine, October 1984: 146-156.

Rossi, Guy. "Cap-Stun." Police Marksman. November-December 1991: 27-31

Sherman, Beth. "A New Recognition of the Realities of Date Rape," New York Times. 23 October 1985: C14

Smith, James A. Rape: Fight Back and Win! New Jersey: Stoeger Publishing Company, 1983.

Smith, Larry Lt. "Chemical Agents for Law Enforcement." Fifth American Society of Law Enforcement Trainers International Training Seminar. January 1992

Southhampton Police Department. How To Prevent Sexual Assault.

State of New York, Department of Social Services. SAY NO!, New York.

Streitfeld, David. " 'Date Rape': The Damage Rises." Washington Post. 24 February 1987: C5

Suffolk County Police Department. Prevent Rape.

Tanner, Morgan. "Fight Back On Four Wheels." Fight Back, Boulder Colorado, Omega Focus Series, May 1986: 51-58

Taylor, Rebecca. "Exercise Improves Your Mood." City Sports Magazine, October 1987: 6-7

Truncale, Joseph Ph.D. Self-Defense For Woman: A Realistic Approach. Rational Press, 1985.

Tzu, Sun. The Art of War. Trans. and intro. Samuel B. Griffith, New York: Oxford University Press, 1963.

United States Army Military Police School. Be Aware Guard Against Rape.

United States Department of Justice. Take a Bite Out of Crime. 1979.

Westheimer, Ruth Dr., Kravetz, Nathan Dr. First Love A Young People's Guide to Sexual Information. New York: Warner Books, 1985: 143-152.

West Palm Beach Police Department Crime Prevention Unit. Sexual Assault.
Zambone, Joe. "Security on the Home Front." Fight Back, Boulder Colorado, Omega Focus Series, May 1986: 64-68.

NOTES

NOTES

NOTES

For a life saving seminar
contact:

Target Consultants Int. Ltd.
P.O. Box 463
Massapequa Park, New York 11762
(516) 541-8092

or in your area